Juicing Recipes

100+ Delicious And Nutritious Green Juicing Recipes That Trim And Slim

Elizabeth Swann

www.Greensmoothies.me

FASTLANE PUBLISHING

Juicing Recipes: 100+ Delicious And Nutritious Green Juicing Recipes That Trim and Slim

Copyright 2013 by Elizabeth Swann
All Rights Reserved

ISBN: 978-965-7636-02-2

Printed In The United States

Contents

Introduction

You might not believe it, but before I tried my first green juice, I felt terribly intimidated because I didn't quite know where to begin. I had purchased my juicer, I had stocked up on all sorts of fruits and vegetables, and I was determined to give green juicing a try. I had heard so many great things about it, yet I felt myself hesitating.

I was nervous about how green juice would taste, even though I always have enjoyed fruits and vegetables of all types. I've never met a fruit or vegetable I didn't like, yet for some reason I was cringing at the idea of juicing.

Are you where I was, so long ago? Are you eager for change in your life, wanting to lose weight, longing for more energy, and desiring a less-stressful existence, yet wondering whether green juicing really is for you? Or could you be charging ahead, excited to cram every vegetable and fruit you can find right down into your juicer and immediately savor the delicious results?

No matter where you are in your life or in your quest for health, I encourage you to pick up this book and start at the beginning. Unlike so many other books that tell you why you need to lose weight, why you need to eliminate stress, and why you ought to be concerned about the way you feel, this book goes above and beyond by explaining exactly *how* powerful green juices can pave the pathway to better health for you now and into the future.

This informative book is brimming with recipes designed to help you create a whole new life, step by step, from the inside out, all with the help of nutritious fruits and vegetables straight from nature's bounty.

If you are ready to lose weight, enjoy higher energy levels than you may have since you were a child, and get better, more restful sleep, it's time for you to start juicing. If you're prepared to say goodbye to stress once and for all, eliminate low-grade depression, and enjoy happiness that radiates from within, you'll be happy to know that green juices can help you to achieve those goals.

If, like so many people, you are tired of looking as though you're aging rapidly, or if you're sick of having dry skin, cracked or peeling fingernails, or brittle hair, you will be thrilled to discover that juicing can help reverse these conditions.

Now that I have experienced the power of green juicing, I know I'll never look back. I have to laugh at myself when I think about how nervous I felt so long ago, before I tried my first green juice. And, I must be gentle with myself at the same time – just as you ought to be kind to yourself. For food manufacturers fill the things we eat with chemicals, artificial sweeteners, fast-acting sugars, and other toxins that only serve to compound our problems. It is not my fault that I didn't know how to eat in the beginning, and it's not your fault if poor eating habits have caused problems for you. What matters is *now*, and what matters is how you treat yourself from this moment into the future.

I urge you to try your first green juice as soon as possible, if you haven't done so already. Moving forward, commit to juicing at least once a day; do it for yourself. The more you juice, the better you'll feel – and like me, you'll discover after a time that you have developed a whole new outlook on life. Let's begin.

Quick note from Liz: A quick word about the recipes in this book. All 60+ recipes are 100% raw, preservative and lactose free which makes them perfect for anyone following a strictly vegan or raw food diet. These flavor packed recipes were created with over 10 years of experience in juicing to ensure ease of use, maximum taste, and absorption and health benefits. So I hope you enjoy drinking them and experience their many amazing health benefits!

You'll easily be able to access the recipes by referring to the table of contents and searching the recipes by health benefit.

Greens: Nature's Gift To Glowing Health

Aside from the vitamins and minerals in green juicing ingredients we use, there is a reason that we should ensure there are greens in every juice we make. That's because greens are full of one of the most important substances on earth: chlorophyll. The same thing that makes trees and plants a bright green color, and imbues our landscape with verdant hues of olive, jade, and emerald is what gives our body the incredible health and vitality that it so deserves.

Why Chlorophyll is King

Many people are not very aware of the benefits of drinking, instead of eating large quantities of chlorophyll. After all, do you really get the minimal seven servings of vegetables that you should have on a daily basis to make sure all your nutrition needs are met? Drinking green juices is a fast and easy way to get all that nutrition -- then some!

Chlorophyll, one of the nutrients of green vegetables is so important to plants that it allows them to convert light into energy they can use to grow, flower and pollinate. In people, chlorophyll has similar benefits. In biochemistry, they call this process the primary photoreceptor pigment. *Green* is King! Chlorophyll is a actually reflected in a blue-green light spectrum range, but we see it as green.

Spinach, a super green food, for example, contains 300 to 600 milligrams per ounce of chlorophyll, whereas olives contain about 1/1000th as much. If you think of some of the healthiest foods on the planet – they are all green:

- Brussels Sprouts
- Kale
- Leaks
- Collard Greens
- Swiss Chard
- Green peas
- Romaine Lettuce
- Turnip Greens
- Wheat Grass
- Barley Grass
- Sea vegetables
- Parsley
- Cilantro
- Basil
- Broccoli
- Bell Peppers
- Asparagus
- Green Cabbage

Now imagine trying to eat large quantities of these life-affirming foods every day. You wouldn't be able to eat much of anything else. The fiber in them would fill you up after just a few servings. Instead, imagine eating ALL of these greens in one day, mixed into super green juices with other ingredients as well. You would have a veritable store-house of nutrition packed into a few glasses of great green juices.

In addition to the specific phytonutrients, minerals and vitamins in each of these foods, they are packed full of chlorophyll. Only greens can give you more chlorophyll and only *green juicing* can really deliver when it comes to super-human health.

Chlorophyll and Your Health

There has been lots of research conducted on chlorophyll and our health. It affects us positively, all the way down to our DNA. That's' quite impressive! It can even repair damaged DNA. It has been shown to decrease the disease of cancer, especially liver and skin cancers, and can also retard the aging process.

Additional Vitamins & Minerals in Green Juices

Just getting high levels of chlorophyll is wonderful, but green juicing also provides a full alphabet soup of vitamins that you need to lose weight, feel beautiful, look amazing, and combat all sorts of diseases. For example:

- Juiced collard and beet greens are full of **vitamin A**. Vitamin A does everything from improve your eyesight to boost your immune system, regulate your genes and to help promote the creation of red blood cells in your body.

- Juiced broccoli and asparagus are full of the entire spectrum of **B vitamins** – called the B complex, including B6. Just this one B vitamin, also called pyridoxine, is responsible for many chemical reactions in the body and is essential for metabolizing food. It helps treat premenstrual symptoms, depression, fatigue, irritability, and brain functioning. Vitamin B2, called riboflavin is important for releasing energy from carbohydrates that you eat. We can juice bok Choy and Brussels sprouts, peas, artichoke and asparagus to get our Vitamin B2. Vitamin B3 or niacin can help with the skin and nerves, as well as help with high blood pressure. We juice artichokes and okra for example, to get more of this great vitamin in our bloodstreams.

- **Vitamin C** is important for helping your immune system as well as detoxing the body from the effects of radiation. It was even used to effectively help the survivors of the recent Fukushima disaster. That's how important this one little vitamin is. It also helps the liver detox the body and reduces the incidence of cancer. And guess what – juiced parsley, broccoli, cauliflower, tomatoes, celery and spinach are full of vitamin C.

- **Vitamin D** is in all leafy green vegetables. This vitamin must be in balance in the body to create healthy bones, to regulate the immune system and to reduce inflammation. Spinach is a great vegetable to add to your green juices to get your vitamin D.

- **Vitamin E and Folate** are the skin beautifiers. Leafy greens come to the rescue again with loads of Vitamin E. Vitamin E also makes sure that your brain cells stay healthy and makes sure to keep 'bad' cholesterol down. Vitamin E is a powerful antioxidant that can prevent certain forms of cancer, too. Kale, collards, spinach and broccoli, are all full of vitamin E and folate.

- **Vitamin F** is found in juiced spirulina, sprouts, wheat germ and flaxseed and sunflower oils. This important, but lesser known vitamin is also known as a healthy fatty acid. Vitamin F is primarily derived from Omega 3 and Omega 6 fatty acids. These are key elements to a high-functioning brain, a great mood, balanced energy levels and even cancer prevention.

- **Vitamin K** is also sometimes called the forgotten vitamin, but it is very important (along with vitamin D) to protect against cardiovascular disease, and loss of bone mass, which can lead to diseases like Osteoporosis. Vitamin K as also proven to reduce the chances of getting certain types of cancer and has been shown to reduce Alzheimer's symptoms as well as reduce someone's tendency to bruise too easily. Vitamin K is juiced in Brussels sprouts, Cabbage, Green Beans, Chives, Collard Greens and Cilantro.

Trace Minerals in Green Juices

Another great reason to green juice is because it is one of the fastest ways to get a load of trace minerals that are so necessary for great health. Minerals are necessary for many reasons. Here are just a few:

- They help to regulate our heartbeat.

- Minerals build strong teeth and bones.

- Minerals help to regulate our hormones – a very important thing to control weight and health.

- Help our bodies grow and replenish old tissue and cells.

- To transmit nerve impulses.

We can get trace minerals from numerous vegetables and fruits, and when we juice them they go straight into the bloodstream so they can start to help us feel absolutely wonderful. Trace minerals we get from green juicing include:

- **Calcium** – available in foods like broccoli, Swiss chard, mustard greens, turnip greens, bok Choy and spinach. Calcium helps to build bones and teeth and prevents Osteoporosis.

- **Manganese** – available in good amounts in lettuces and spinach. Manganese helps to ensure good bone structure, ensures that calcium is absorbed properly, supports the functioning of the thyroid gland, regulates blood sugar levels, metabolizes fats and carbohydrates and makes sure our sex hormones are excreted properly.

- **Iodine** – available in kelp and other sea plants, as well as strawberries, beans, and cruciform vegetables like cauliflower and broccoli, this mineral can help prevent thyroid disease.

- **Zinc** – this essential mineral is great for the immune system and helps to prevent hair loss in balanced amounts. At also helps to regulate testosterone production. Zinc is in palm hearts and cabbage, lemongrass and sprouts.

- **Sulphur** – Onions, cabbage and broccoli are great to juice to make sure you are getting enough sulphur. Sulphur is a potent antioxidant and anti-cancer mineral. It can also help prevent the cells from absorbing heavy metals.

- **Phosphorous** – Phosphorous also helps in bone formation, hormonal balance, energy production, and cell repair and nutrient absorption. Phosphorous is one of the most important and predominant minerals in the body. Without enough phosphorous you can suffer from bone decay, tooth decay, and rickets along with a compromised immune system. Fortunately when you juice watermelon, squash, pumpkin, or add ground flax seed to your green juices, you get plenty of phosphorous.

- **Iron** – Many green leafy vegetables, sprouts and fruits are full of iron. This mineral is responsible for maintaining muscle function, and making sure the blood is healthy. Iron also support brain function and protects against anemia, or iron-poor blood which can cause weakness.

- **Copper** – Copper is important for all our connective tissues. It keeps our eyes and hair healthy and

- **Selenium** – Selenium is very important for fighting weakness and fatigue. It can be found in brown rice, but also in trace amounts in vegetables like spinach. An ideal dose of selenium is about w

Elizabeth's 8 Step Process For Creating the Perfect Green Juice Every Single Time!

With all the health benefits of green juicing I know you are as excited as I am about getting right down to building your own green juices from start to finish. This chapter will discuss exactly how to prepare, and consume green juices. It's a really easy process when you know how to do it right.

Here are 8 simple steps to follow:

1. Figure out your goal for green juicing. Are you just starting out? Do you want to lose weight, or boost energy? Are you just trying to get more nutrients in your body or are you going for a full detox program? Are you trying to help naturally cure a specific health issue like acne, or high blood pressure? Knowing these things before you choose your green juice will help you to pick ingredients that are meant just for you, and your own specific needs. Remember that those needs may change over time. That's why this guide is so helpful. You might start out wanting to lose weight with green juicing and then later on, decide you can incorporate some special juices to facilitate an intense workout-training program or to help you cram for late night exams.

Do you need an afternoon boost to help keep up with your kids? How about a nerve tonic to help you distress? Green juicing does it all, so learning what each ingredient does for you over time can be very beneficial.

2. Make sure you choose a good juicer or blender to do the job. We'll talk more about this is an upcoming chapter, but having the right tools can make your juice habit much easier to stick with.

3. Start with leafy greens. The primary ingredient of almost any green juice is – you guessed it – green! You can choose from spinach, Swiss chard, different lettuces, kale, and more. The leafy greens are all full of numerous vitamins and minerals and can do everything from support weight loss, to boost energy and prevent many forms of diseases from Diabetes to Heart Disease to poor eyesight, and even depression. Always choose organic leafy greens so that you don't drink a glass full of pesticides and herbicides used in conventional farming. You can visit your local farmer's market or get your greens from a grocery store. You can also grow them yourself. Leafy greens are really easy to grow in containers in a sunny area of your own home, and they can grow all year long. If you have a garden already, congratulations, now you can start juicing your greens!

4. Add a few more alkaline vegetables. This can be as diverse as cabbage, broccoli, cauliflower, carrots, and even sweet potato. You can juice beets, celery, and cucumbers; as well as herbs like cilantro, basil, rosemary, or thyme. Almost any vegetable that has high water content can be juiced.

5. Spice it up with ginger or onions for certain green juicing recipes. Both of these juicing options have a very strong taste, but highly medicinal qualities, so you may want to start by adding just a touch to your sweeter juices (like those that contain apples or carrots) and then experiment with adding higher quantities later on.

6. Peel, or cut up vegetables that need to be put through the juicer and then put it all through the juicer to be juiced.

7. Top off with a squeeze of lemon, which will help to keep the juice from oxidizing, a fancy word that describes what happens to living matter, like fruits and vegetables, when they are exposed to oxygen. The more a juice oxidizes, the less its nutrients are available for the body to assimilate, so it is best to consume your green juices immediately after they have been juiced. While this isn't always possible, we will discuss ways to store green juices effectively a little later on, plus we'll go over a few juicers that have lower spin rates, so they tend to incorporate

less oxygen into the green juice. If you have ever added lime or lemon to guacamole for a party to keep it from turning brown, you are essentially doing the same thing – keeping the avocados from oxidizing.

8. Serve immediately with a few ice cubes or if you have made a very strong-tasting juice, you can water it down a bit with purified water. If you are serving the juice later, refrigerate it right away.

It's that easy! Green juicing can be fun and variable, and you'll start to feel immediate rewards from doing it, so let's move on to storing green juices for the times you can't juice and drink them right away. We all have busy lives, and sometimes you can't juice when you would want to, so let's figure out exactly how to juice more often by storing our juices properly.

How to Make Green Juice in a Blender

If you just can't get your hands on a juicer, this section will be vital.

If you are using a blender or Vitamix, you will be consuming more of the fiber of the fruits and vegetables that you juice. Don't' expect them to have the same consistency as those green juices made in one of the juicers discussed earlier that extracts the fiber form the fruit or vegetable. You can still get an amazing smoothie from a blender though, and you can even throw in some ice or rice milk, almond milk or wheat grass powder to make your green smoothie extra refreshing and health-boosting.

Don't prepare your fruits or vegetables too soon. Make sure you only cut them up or skin them right before you use them, because this is the food's natural protection against bacteria and oxidation.

You will want to skin all fruits and vegetables, and remove seeds if you are using large-seeded fruits. Things like strawberries are fine to leave as is – just cut the tops of the greens off, if you like, but you can also leave them in-tact and just throw everything in your blender. You may also want to cut the stalks of kale leaves, since they won't blend as well. It is also important to add a little liquid, even if it is just purified water or organic apple cider vinegar to make sure your hard foods blend well.

Make sure you place foods in the blender, lightest to heaviest, since the heavier foods will tend to sink to the bottom anyway. If you are using a blender you can use citrus to help flavor your juice, just be mindful of your 2 to 1 ratio of vegetables over fruits for the healthiest green juice. If you are using a lemon, be sure to peel the skin – the same goes with all other citrus. Also core apples – to remove seeds and stems.

Cut the fruit and vegetables into small enough pieces to tumble around in your blender and be completely liquefied. Add some lemon to keep the juice from oxidizing and enjoy. It's that simple.

Green Juices: The Perfect Food for Weight Loss

Whether you're just starting with green juicing or if you've been enjoying green juices for some time now, you may be considering using these tasty, nutritious juices as weapons in your battle against excess weight.

Before I really get into how to use green juices for weight loss, let me just make one thing very clear. When it comes to losing weight the healthy way, there's no such thing as a miracle cure. It's important that you recognize that those pounds and inches took some time to accumulate, and that they're not going to disappear overnight. Just as with any other healthy eating plan, you've got to give green juices the time they need to do their work inside your body.

Before you begin feeling discouraged and wondering just *how long* it's going to take you to lose weight with green juices, I'll let you in on a secret: Of all diet plans out there, the ones that incorporate lots of green juices are among the most successful. They're also among the easiest to follow, because when you're feeding your body right, giving your cells the nutrition they need, and focusing on getting high-quality nutrition each and every time you take in food, you never feel deprived.

What makes green juice the perfect food for weight loss? Here, in no particular order, are the top three reasons it works so well:

- ⮑ The modern diet is filled with foods that are high in fat and calories, but low in actual nutrition. Green juices are the opposite of the processed foods that might make up your diet now – they're low in calories and contain very little fat if any, and they are brimming with the best nutrition available. Your body never believes it is starving when you're enjoying green juices, so it releases weight rapidly.

- Many diet plans are low in calories, but they don't provide you with enough nutrients to feel energetic and enthusiastic about your weight loss program. Most of us have been in the position of going on a crash diet, losing a few pounds, and then giving up simply because we're lacking in energy. It all comes back to nutrition here – green juices have all the nutrition you need to feel great. In fact, most people who start a green juicing regimen and stick with it notice that they feel better than they may have felt in many years.

- While it's true that your fat stores will provide you with calories to burn, those calories are often toxic. This is because the body actually *stores toxins* in your fat cells – and when those cells melt away, toxins are released into your system. These toxins make you feel sluggish, grouchy, and unmotivated. If all you're doing is following a low-calorie diet plan, your body will do all it can to hang onto the fat and the toxins that fat contains. With green juices, you flush toxins from your system as you lose weight. Add even a little exercise into the equation, and you start rebuilding your body from the inside out.

It's understandable that you might be feeling nervous, skeptical, or worried that green juices might not work for you. But by replacing at least one meal per day with a healthy green juice, you'll soon lay those feelings aside and replace them with excitement, joyfulness, and a renewed lease on life.

Are you ready to begin losing weight? While any of the recipes in this book can be an excellent addition to a healthy weight loss plan, the green juices that follow are perfect for weight loss. Drinking them frequently will help you get off to a great start.

Green Classic

4 medium carrots
1 whole cucumber
3 leaves kale
1/4 green bell pepper

Wash all ingredients well. Remove the seeds and stem from the green bell pepper, then juice all vegetables together.

Potassium-Rich Energy Juice

    4 medium carrots
    1 celery stalk, long fibers removed
    1 apple, any type
    1 handful whole, fresh parsley
    1 handful whole, fresh spinach leaves
    1/2 lemon, peeled

Wash all produce well, and then process in juicer.

Calcium Bone Builder Juice

    1/2 cup fresh broccoli florets
    3 medium carrots
    1 apple
    1 small handful whole, fresh parsley
    1/2 lemon, peeled

Wash all produce well, and then process in juicer.

Weight Loss Kick-Start Greenie

    2 handfuls fresh, whole spinach
    1 medium cucumber
    2 stalks celery, long fibers removed
    1/2 inch section fresh ginger root, scrubbed and peeled
    1 small bunch whole parsley
    2 apples, your choice
    1 lime, peeled
    1/2 lemon, peeled

Wash all produce well, and then process in juicer.

Refreshing Celery-Ginger Juice

    1 bunch of cilantro
    1 large Granny Smith apple, cut in quarters with stem removed
    8 celery stalks, long fibers removed
    1 inch section ginger root, peeled
    ¼ lemon, peeled

Wash all produce well, and then process in juicer.

ABC Juice

2 medium apples, any type
2 beets, peeled and cut into quarters
4 medium carrots
7 leaves Swiss chard
1 inch section ginger root, peeled

Wash all produce well, and then process in juicer. Delicious over ice.

Carrot-Watercress Juice

1 clove garlic (2 if you prefer a stronger flavor)
5 large carrots
½ bunch of parsley
1 large handful watercress
1 small apple, any type (eliminate if you like sharp, savory tastes.)

Wash all produce well, and then process in juicer.

Carrot-Parsnip Juice

1 medium parsnip
4 medium carrots

Wash all produce well, and then process in juicer. Fantastic over ice.

Savory Caesar Salad Juice

8 leaves Romaine lettuce
1 medium parsnip
4 small to medium carrots
1 clove garlic (2 if you prefer a stronger flavor)

Wash all produce well, and then process in juicer. Delicious for lunch or dinner.

Cucumber Dandy Delight

1 large handful dandelion leaves
½ head broccoli, including florets and stalks
2 celery stalks, long fibers removed
1 small cucumber

Wash all produce well, and then process in juicer.

Detox Made Delightful: Green Juices for Cleansing

Whether you detoxify your body on a regular basis or if you're only now beginning to understand the importance of regular detoxification, you'll be thrilled to discover that juicing offers a fast, easy route to total body detox. Better than pills, better than "Hollywood" cleanses, and certainly better than coffee enemas and some of the other crazy detox methods out there, green juices detoxify your body from the inside out.

Green juices have a powerful cleansing effect on the body – you may know that much already. What you might not be aware of is exactly *how* green juices do their work, detoxifying and cleansing you from the inside out.

It all begins on a cellular level. Because fresh green juices are so rich in nutrients, and because they are alkaline rather than acidic, they prompt your body's cells to finally release the toxic loads that they may have been carrying for months, years, or even decades.

As toxins are released from your body's cells and replaced with vitamins, minerals, and important enzymes, they are then removed via the many elimination channels the body possesses. These include:

- ➲ The lungs – You'll notice that when you're in the midst of detoxifying your body, your breath smells terrible and you might even get a nasty taste in your mouth.

- ➲ The kidneys – Your kidneys have the important task of purifying your blood. They remove massive loads of toxins from the bloodstream during detoxification, which is why it's so important to drink plenty of water and keep pouring those fresh vegetable juices into your system.

⮑ The skin – We often forget that the skin is the body's largest organ – and it's a major route for detoxification. Many people notice that their sweat smells worse during detox, and it is not at all uncommon for breakouts to occur, particularly if you've been living with a diet that subjects your body to a steady stream of toxins.

When you give your body green juices filled with living enzymes that aid the digestive process, you may also notice the effects of detoxification in another way – old built-up sludge from your colon may send you to the restroom more frequently than usual for a few days. While this might seem inconvenient, you are very likely to notice that you've lost a few pounds and your belly is flatter after just a few days of detoxifying.

By giving your body optimal nutrition from green juices that contain powerful enzymes capable of breaking down toxins, you allow your cells to function properly. Instead of straining under a heavy toxic load, the body's cells work efficiently after detoxification. They process oxygen more effectively, and they heal themselves rapidly. Nutrients move through the body with speed, rapidly making their way to all the tissues, bones, and fibers that make up your being. All this sounds miraculous, doesn't it? The fact is, it's simple science – not magic or a miracle. Feed your body what it needs, eliminate toxins, and you'll enjoy a healthier life. It's truly a recipe for success.

While you can enjoy any green juice during detoxification, the following recipes are designed to help speed the process along. Drink as many of these juices as you can each day and remember to eliminate harmful foods and other nasty substances from your daily routine. Before you know it, you'll be feeling like a brand new version of you!

Note: For an extra boost, stir a superfood supplement into your juice before consuming it. Some great ones to try include wheatgrass, barley grass, or blue-green algae (spirulina) powder.

Sweet and Sour Detox Delight

2 apples, quartered with stems removed
4 celery stalks, long fibers removed
1 medium cucumber
5 leaves kale
¼ to 1/2 lemon, zest removed
1 inch ginger root, peeled

Wash all produce well, and then process in juicer.

Spinach-Parsley Perfection

4 medium carrots
3 stalks celery, long fibers removed
1 large handful spinach
½ cucumber
1 small handful parsley, rinsed well

Wash all produce well, and then process in juicer.

Spicy Mustard Mixup

1 small handful of mustard greens (Feel free to add more if you like the taste.)
5 large carrots
2 celery stalks, long fibers removed

Wash all produce well, and then process in juicer. If the taste is too strong for you, cut with water or add a cucumber to the mix.

Simply Refreshing

5 celery stalks, long fibers removed
1 small cucumber

Wash all produce well, and then process in juicer. This is wonderful over ice.

Green Dandy

2 kale leaves
1 small handful of dandelion leaves
4 medium carrots

Wash all produce well, and then process in juicer.

Superbly Smooth Green Detox Juice

3 celery stalks, long fibers removed
1 medium cucumber
3 kale leaves
1 handful parsley, rinsed well
1 lime, peeled (nice with lemon, too)
1 medium apple or pear

Wash all produce well, and then process in juicer.

Fantastically Fruity Detox Drink

1 small handful spinach

3 kale leaves

1 cup fresh pineapple chunks

2 large apples, any type

½ lemon, peeled (Try a Meyer lemon – this variety is sweeter and more fragrant than other types.)

Wash all produce well, and then process in juicer.

Super-Green Detox Machine

1 handful spinach

3 kale leaves

1 small handful dandelion greens

1 handful parsley, rinsed well

1 handful fresh alfalfa sprouts

1 large cucumber

3 yellow or green pears

1 lime, zest removed

Wash all produce well, and then process in juicer. Fantastic over ice!

Cucumber-Beet Blast

1 medium cucumber

1 medium beet, peeled and quartered

2 large or 3 medium carrots

2 celery stalks, long fibers removed

1 small handful parsley, rinsed well

½ lemon, peeled

Wash all produce well, and then process in juicer.

Clean Green Cucumber

1 large cucumber

1 large handful spinach

1 bunch parsley, rinsed well

1 stalk celery, long fibers removed

1/2 lemon, peeled

Wash all produce well, and then process in juicer.

Stress Management the Green Juice Way

No matter who you are or what your circumstances in life, it's quite likely that you carry stress with you. While a certain amount of stress can help keep you feeling motivated and competitive, it isn't good to feel stressed all the time! Luckily, consuming plenty of green juices can help you to combat stress and manage feelings of tension from the inside out.

Maybe you already know that green juices are an outstanding tool for fighting stress. The question is, do you know why they work so well? There are a few reasons why green juices help the body and mind to relax:

Fresh green juices contain high levels of minerals and other nutrients that help to alleviate stress. For example, juices with high magnesium and calcium can help to promote feelings of calm.

Juices with high levels of antioxidants including vitamins A and C help knock stress out. Lettuce juice, with its many nutrients, acts as a mild sedative that promotes almost immediate relaxation.

Certain superfoods help to alleviate stress. For example, peppermint and spearmint essential oils add refreshing flavor to juices while calming the mind and soothing nerves.

It's definitely important to note here that you've got to get into a good green juicing habit and enjoy those green juices at least once daily, if not more often, to really reap the stress-reducing benefits they provide. In the last two chapters, you learned how the nutrients in fresh green juices bring your cells back to health from the inside out; the same nutrients are the ones that are going to help you to eliminate excess stress from your daily life.

Like juicing for weight loss and juicing to detoxify your body, juicing for stress reduction works best when you eliminate toxic foods and other harmful substances from your daily diet. If you smoke or drink alcohol in an attempt to stop stress, I urge you to quit these habits and replace them with green juices. Yes, you may miss them for a short period of time, but just think how much better you'll feel each day once they are gone from your life for good!

Providing your body with the powerful phytonutrients that green juices contain promotes healthy mental balance. Juicing approximately 10 servings of vegetables and fruits daily, and maintaining this habit for life, will help you to become a calmer, more serene person with a more positive outlook on life.

There's one more way eliminating toxic stress with green juices will help you. Are you aware that excessive stress loads tax the immune system? Over time, your tendency to become ill increases when you are overly stressed, and as you succumb to one sickness after another, your immune system becomes depleted. Not only will green juicing help you to eliminate that stress, it will boost your immune system so you'll ultimately be more productive, more effective at work or parenting, and just so much healthier.

The best, most effective, most direct way to provide your body and mind with the essential nutrients they need is by juicing a wide variety of vegetables and fruits each and every day. Are you ready to feel the difference? Enjoy these ten fantastic stress-busting juice recipes and discover the calmer, healthier you that's longing to emerge.

Veg-Out Veggie Juice

1 head Bibb lettuce
1 small cucumber
2 celery stalks, long fibers removed
4 carrots
1 small apple

Wash all produce well, and then process in juicer. Pour over ice, and sip slowly.

Relaxing Lettuce Lemonade

6 lettuce leaves (Romaine or Bibb will do nicely)
2 celery stalks, long strands removed
½ medium cucumber
1 lemon, peeled
2 apples, quartered

Wash all produce well, and then process in juicer.

Cabbage Chiller

1/4 small green cabbage
5 carrots
1 small cucumber

Wash all produce well, and then process in juicer.

Relaxing Mineral Tonic

½ small beetroot, peeled and cut into large chunks
2 celery stalks, long strands removed
2 medium carrots

Wash all produce well, and then process in juicer.

Carrot-Cabbage Tension Tamer

¼ small cabbage (red or green, your choice)
6 medium carrots

Wash all produce well, and then process in juicer.

Calming Kale Cooler

3 kale leaves, ribs removed
1 sliced mango
1 cup fresh pineapple chunks

Wash all produce well, and then process in juicer.

Veggie Revolution

1 large handful spinach
2 medium carrots
1 ripe tomato (use a cucumber instead of you prefer)
1 medium apple

Wash all produce well, and then process in juicer.

Light Green Citrus Chiller

- 1 small head romaine lettuce
- 1 handful of kale, ribs removed
- 2 medium carrots
- 1 cucumber
- 2 large oranges, peeled
- 1 small lemon, peeled

Wash all produce well, and then process in juicer.

Sweet Apple Greenie

- 2 green apples
- 1 cucumber
- 3 kale leaves
- 6 romaine lettuce leaves
- 1 inch ginger root, peeled

Wash all produce well, and then process in juicer.

Garden Delight

- 20 green grapes
- 2 medium Carrots
- 1 large handful spinach
- 2 medium apples
- 1 cucumber
- 1 mild green bell pepper
- 1 medium tomato (optional)

Wash all produce well, and then process in juicer.

Boosting Your Mood with Green Juices

At some point, everyone goes through feelings of sadness; often, these feelings are persistent and lead to depression, or a case of "the blues." All too often, we turn to fatty, salty, or sweet comfort foods in an attempt to bring ourselves up out of the doldrums; this tactic backfires, and soon enough, we're feeling worse than we did in the first place.

Depression is a physical problem as well as an emotional one. Here are some signs that it might be affecting you:

- ⮑ Insomnia – Difficulty sleeping can be a sign of depression.

- ⮑ Poor concentration – If you're having difficulty focusing at work or even on your favorite hobbies, you may be experiencing depression, particularly if your lack of concentration is accompanied by additional symptoms.

- ⮑ Feeling down – If you feel like all the fun has gone out of life and you're just not as enthusiastic as you once were, it's very likely that depression is manifesting itself in your life.

- ⮑ Low immunity – Do you become ill frequently? Are you plagued by aches, pains, and headaches, sniffles, coughing, and other minor physical ailments? The stress depression causes could be putting excess strain on your immune system.

Shifting your nutritional intake into high gear can bring about huge changes in the way you feel – and those changes can happen rapidly. As with other positive changes brought on by green juices, they begin on the inside, the moment you begin to drench your body's cells with the many concentrated nutrients powerful green juices contain. Some of the best juice recipes for improving mood include the following ingredients and/or nutrients:

B vitamins – Foods high in vitamin B include leafy greens and whole, sprouted grains such as barley and alfalfa seeds. B vitamins help improve nerve function, so your brain begins to clear itself of the mental fog depression brings with it.

Omega-3 Fatty Acids – Chia seeds, flax, and walnuts are three superfoods that contain omega-3 fatty acids. While you can't put them into your juice, you can add them to your salad, put them in a green smoothie made with fresh green juice, a banana, and the boost of your choice, or just nibble on them throughout the day. Omega-3 fatty acids support important brain chemicals including dopamine and serotonin.

Foods and herbs that support serotonin production – Fish like salmon, raw cacao nibs, and cocoa powder are examples of foods your brain loves. If you choose to consume chocolate, avoid milk chocolate and watch out for candies that have a lot of added sugar. These things can backfire on you and make your problems worse.

Herbs and essential oils that encourage relaxation and promote healthy sleep are excellent additions to green juices and herbal teas. Valerian, lemon balm, St. John's wort, lavender, and borage are all examples of herbs that help to battle depression and bring on healthy balance within the brain.

Now that you know more about how enjoying green juices on a regular basis will help improve your moods and give you a better outlook on life even if you feel ok now, you're probably eager to try a recipe or two. Here are ten fantastic mood-elevating green juice recipes. Go ahead and take a break – try one right now!

Ginger-Lime Joy

1 celery stalk, long fibers removed
2 large apples, quartered
1 kiwi fruit, peeled
1 small handful parsley, rinsed well
1 inch-long section ginger root, peeled
½ lime, peeled

Wash all produce well, and then process in juicer.

Cilantro Shot

1 bunch cilantro, rinsed well
½ lime, peeled
½ teaspoon sea salt
3 ounces purified water

Wash all produce well, and then process in juicer.

Inspirational Citrus Greenie

6 kale leaves
6 Swiss chard leaves
1 medium cucumber
6 small tangerines or clementines

Juice and enjoy over ice! Wash all produce well, and then process in juicer.

Chlorophyll Cooler

2 medium kale leaves
2 celery stalks, long fibers removed
4 stems parsley, rinsed well
3 large carrots
1 medium to large apple

Wash all produce well, and then process in juicer.

Therapy in a Glass

1 large handful spinach, washed well
1 medium beet, peeled and quartered
2 apples, any type

Wash all produce well, and then process in juicer.

Feeling Fine Fruits and Greens

handful of lettuce leaves
1 yellow or green pear
10 ripe strawberries
1/2 lemon, scrubbed, with zest left on
1 large apple, quartered

Wash all produce well, and then process in juicer.

Not so Mean Green Machine

1 medium cucumber
5 kale leaves
4 celery stalks, long fibers removed
1/2 lemon, scrubbed, with zest left on
½ inch section ginger root, peeled
2 apples, your choice

Wash all produce well, and then process in juicer. Fantastic over ice.

Blues-Bursting Berry Juice

1 handful of spinach
1 ½ cups fresh blueberries
1 medium apple
1 lemon, peeled

Wash all produce well, and then process in juicer.

Perky Pear

3 yellow or green pears
1 medium cucumber
1 handful spinach
3 kale leaves
1/2 lemon, peeled
12 pods sugar snap peas

Wash all produce well, and then process in juicer.

Pineapple Mint Power Greenie

1/3 pineapple
8 Bibb lettuce leaves
2 sprigs fresh mint

Ready to Work Out? Release Your Inner Athlete with Green Juices

Green juices are wonderfully beneficial for anyone, but they're even more helpful to people who are working to increase fitness. By nourishing your body properly, you help yourself in a number of ways:

- Healthy cells generate new ones faster

- Cells that are healthy repair themselves rapidly

- Green juices help you remain hydrated

- The nutrients green juices contain help to support energetic exercise, encourage muscle development, and reduce the potential for the inflammation and oxidation some people experience with exercise.

If you're overweight, feeling tired and groggy, and dealing with excessive stress in your life – all things we've talked about eliminating with powerful green juices – exercise is something you need to add to your routine to help speed things along and bring your body and mind back into balance. Unfortunately, many of us dread exercise; but with green juices, this can change. Consume these marvelously nutritious drinks each day, and you'll soon discover that your body longs to be in motion.

Drinks manufacturers add bright artificial colors to their beverages, along with sweeteners (caloric or artificial) plus, they often add B vitamins, minerals, and electrolytes to their products to aid in rehydration. The question is this: Why spend money on overpriced bottled drinks, when healthy green juices contain everything your body needs? Much more nutritious than sports drinks, the healthy beverages support workouts and recovery in several ways:

- Fruits and vegetables are natural sources of electrolytes. Those containing high levels of potassium, such as carrots, sweet potato, and cantaloupe help to alleviate muscle cramps and fatigue. As a bonus, they also help to prevent and alleviate headaches.

- Leafy greens that contain high levels of magnesium help to prevent muscle cramps. Some winners are Swiss chard, spinach, and kale.

- Juices high in vitamin C, such as those made with broccoli, kiwi fruit, spinach, oranges, and other citrus fruits help boost workouts by keeping your immune system healthy. You'll get fit faster – and you'll stay that way – if you can avoid minor illnesses that sap you of your energy and deplete your strength.

- Surprise! Green juices are high in protein. Every sixteen ounces of green juice you consume contains about 5 grams of protein – that's more than you'll find in a large egg white, which contains about 3.6 grams of protein. Protein helps build strong muscles and body tissues, so drink up. Superfood boosts like pea protein powder, chia seeds, and hemp protein powder can take your juices to the next level.

The fact that green juices help the body release excess weight and eliminate toxins helps with overall fitness, too. A lighter, leaner body is less prone to injury, and being at a healthy weight while exercising is truly a joy. Finally, it's well worth mentioning that exercising on its own is great, but exercising with the help of powerful green juices is fantastic. The more juices you feast on, the more you'll speed your progress and the faster you'll release your inner athlete – he or she is longing to emerge!

While any green juice will nourish your body and help you feel fantastic, some juices really do a great job of helping you take your exercise routine to a whole new level. Here are ten delicious recipes to help you get started.

Kickin' Kale Greenie

    3 medium carrots
    1 large apple
    4 celery stalks, long fibers removed
    8 kale leaves

Wash all produce well, and then process in juicer.

Bodybuilder's Green Delight

5 kale leaves
1 large bunch parsley, rinsed well
10 romaine lettuce leaves
1 medium to large cucumber
2 celery stalks, long fibers removed
1 medium apple or pear

Wash all produce well, and then process in juicer.

Bright Green Power Blend

2 celery stalks, long fibers removed
1 medium cucumber
1 green or yellow apple
1/2 lemon, peeled
½ inch section ginger root, scrubbed and peeled
1 green chard leaf
1 small handful cilantro
4 kale leaves
1 handful spinach

Wash all produce well, and then process in juicer.

Sweet Fennel Body Boost

½ fennel bulb, with greens if you prefer
1 medium apple
2 large carrots
¼ beet, peeled and cut into two chunks

Wash all produce well, and then process in juicer.

Veggie Power

1 handful parsley, rinsed well
½ small cucumber
2 asparagus stalks (feed into juicer bottom first)
4 medium carrots

Wash all produce well, and then process in juicer.

Post-Workout Pick Me Up

3 large carrots
1 handful spinach
1/6 head green cabbage
½ inch section ginger root, scrubbed and peeled (optional)

Wash all produce well, and then process in juicer.

Green Apple Power Blend

2 small handfuls spinach
3 kale leaves
2 green or yellow apples
1 medium cucumber
6 to 7 stems fresh parsley, rinsed well
1 lemon, peeled
1 inch section ginger root, scrubbed and peeled (optional)

Wash all produce well, and then process in juicer.

Healing Aloe Greenie

¼ cup raw aloe juice or 2 large stalks aloe from living plant
1 celery stalk, long fibers removed
1 medium carrot
1 medium apple
1 small handful dandelion greens
1 small handful parsley, rinsed well
¼ head green cabbage
½ inch fresh ginger root, scrubbed and peeled

Pour aloe in glass, if using juice. Wash all produce well, and then process in juicer. Add to aloe, stir well, and enjoy.

Post-Workout Recovery Greenie

1½ pounds of greens, particularly fresh wild ones if available – look for miner's lettuce, dandelion, chick weed, sow thistle, or yellow dock
1 small cucumber
6 celery stalks, long fibers removed
4 bok choi leaves
1 lemon, peeled
1 inch section fresh ginger root, scrubbed and peeled

Wash all produce well, and then process in juicer.

Bok Choi Root Boost

2 medium carrots
1 large beet, peeled and cut into large chunks
1 large sweet potato, peeled if not organic
1/2 inch section ginger root, scrubbed and peeled
1 medium-sized head baby bok choi
5 strawberries

Wash all produce well, and then process in juicer.

Beautiful from the Inside Out: Green Juices for Skin and Nails

We've all seen those people – you know – the ones with glowing skin and strong, healthy fingernails. They have an effortlessly attractive look, and their beauty seems to shine from the inside out. Now that you've reached the middle of this book, you know how green juices can help you to lose weight, eliminate stress, fight depression, and even help make exercise more effective; what you may not know is that powerful green juices will give you that healthy glow you so admire in others.

There are several reasons why green juices help impart natural beauty:

- Leafy greens are brimming with nutrition. They are like miniature storehouses of vitamins and minerals, including vitamins C, E, and K; plus they contain high levels of B vitamins. These are essential for healthy, beautiful skin and nails.

- Living plants contain chemicals known as phytonutrients. These tiny, naturally occurring compounds include lutein and beta carotene, both of which aid in warding off cellular damage that comes with age. The chlorophyll these plants contain helps to keep blood cells fresh and clean, plus it stimulates the production of new, healthy blood cells. Great blood flow leads to superb skin.

- Fruits and vegetables are wonderfully rich in minerals, including calcium, iron, magnesium, and potassium. They also contain high levels of amino acids. All these substances help build strong, firm tissues including strong fingernails and healthy skin cells.

⮑ Leafy greens and other fresh plants have an alkalizing effect on the body which helps to eliminate the harmful effects acidizing foods can have. If you have consumed alcohol, cheese, meat, chocolate, or coffee in the past, or if you continue to consume them now, they could be making you look (and feel) older and less vibrant. Replacing these substances with life-giving fruits and vegetables will help to bring your body's pH level back into balance so you feel and look fantastic.

It's worth mentioning here that the fresher your leafy greens and other juice ingredients are, the healthier they are for you. Ideally, we would all grow our own greens and harvest them just before juicing; however, shopping for the freshest organic fruits and vegetables you can find will help to ensure you get the highest nutrient levels possible.

This is important, because just as pasteurization kills the enzymes that make green juices so powerful, a long stay on the kitchen counter or inside the refrigerator can do the same thing. Always look for the freshest produce, which grocers usually put behind older stock on shelves. Visit local farmers markets if possible, and don't be afraid to strike up conversations with the farmers you meet there. Many of these people provide organic produce at local markets not just because they enjoy making a living by farming, but because they hold a strong belief that the fruits and vegetables they produce contribute to healthier land for farming, a healthier planet overall, and healthier people. Perhaps you can offer to buy in bulk and save a bit of money on your juicing ingredients. It never hurts to ask, and you may just make a new friend or two in the process.

The bottom line is this: The fresher the fruits and vegetables you consume, the healthier you are going to be, and the better your skin and nails are going to look. The more green juices you drink, the faster you'll achieve the results you desire. Remember to keep drinking green juices, and you'll maintain your looks in years to come. Here are ten fantastic recipes to help you get started.

Green Grapefruit Juice

1 medium apple
1 grapefruit, peeled
4 celery stalks, long fibers removed
4 kale leaves
1 medium cucumber
1 lime, peeled

Wash all produce well, and then process in juicer.

Green Tonic

2 medium green apples, such as Granny Smith
2 handfuls spinach
6 Swiss chard leaves
1 medium cucumber
4 celery stalks, long fibers removed
1/2 bulb fennel
1 small bunch basil, rinsed well

Wash all produce well, and then process in juicer.

Ginger-Lemon Greenie

2 medium apples
1/6 head green cabbage
2 large carrots
1 inch section ginger root, scrubbed and peeled
5 Swiss chard leaves
1/4 lemon, peeled

Wash all produce well, and then process in juicer.

Vibrancy Greenie

1 medium parsnip
¼ medium turnip, scrubbed well and peeled if not organic
1 small handful turnip greens
3 celery stalks, long fibers removed
2 to 4 medium apples, your choice
1 inch section ginger root, scrubbed and peeled (optional)

Wash all produce well, and then process in juicer.

Beauty from Within

1 medium yellow or green pear
3 kale leaves
1 medium yellow or green apple
1 small cucumber

Wash all produce well, and then process in juicer.

Fresh-Faced Greenie

 1 small cucumber
 1/4 honeydew melon, seeded and cut into chunks
 10 seedless green grapes
 2 kiwi fruits, skins removed
 1 handful spinach
 1 lemon, peeled
 1 sprig of mint (optional)

Wash all produce well, and then process in juicer. Fantastic over ice.

Inner Spark Greenie

 1 large handful spinach
 2 large carrots
 ¼ fresh pineapple, skinned and cut into chunks
 1 small handful cilantro, rinsed well
 1 lime, peeled
 1 pinch cayenne pepper (optional)

Wash all produce well, and then process in juicer. After pouring into glass, add cayenne and stir well. Enjoy over ice.

Chlorophyll Cooler

 1 small handful parsley, rinsed well
 3 kale leaves
 1 firm kiwi fruit, skinned
 1 medium green apple, such as Granny Smith
 2 celery stalks, long fibers removed (Optional)

Wash all produce well, and then process in juicer.

Rainbow Veggie Super Burst

1 small beet, peeled and quartered
1 large carrot
1 red bell pepper, seeded
1 red or yellow apple, quartered
3 celery stalks, long fibers removed
1 small handful cilantro, rinsed well
2 kale leaves
5 basil leaves
1 small tomato
1 inch ginger root, scrubbed and peeled
1 inch section daikon radish
1 pinch turmeric powder

Wash all produce well, and then process in juicer. Sprinkle turmeric powder into finished juice and stir well. Enjoy over ice.

Fennel Facial in a Glass

1 bulb fennel with greens
3 kale leaves
1 small head Bibb lettuce
2 stalks celery, long fibers removed
1 lemon (try leaving the peel on if it's organic)
1 medium green or yellow apple

Wash all produce well, and then process in juicer. Pour over ice and sip slowly.

Growing Beautiful Hair: Green Juices to the Rescue

Whether you're a woman who desires long, lovely locks, or if you're a man who's beginning to see the signs of male pattern baldness, or if you're somewhere in-between, you'll be thrilled to discover that drinking plenty of fresh green juices can help you to grow better, stronger hair – and do it faster, too.

Just like other body tissues, hair is composed of protein. Have you ever seen someone who is undernourished or who has been consuming a poor diet comprised mostly of processed junk food? When the body is deprived or proper nourishment, the hair is one of the first things to go. It becomes brittle, lifeless, and weak; it starts to break off, and it begins to get thinner. The nutrients that the body would normally earmark for hair growth are instead sent to bones, muscles, the brain, the eyes, and the inner organs – things that are necessary for survival.

By now, you're well aware of the power green juices have to nourish every single cell of the body from the inside out. Once the body's most important structures are properly nourished, healthy hair growth will resume in earnest. It's not uncommon for people who begin juicing to experience thicker, longer, fuller hair – even when that's not what they set out to accomplish in the beginning.

There are a few ways that fresh green juices help hair to grow strong and healthy:

- Leafy greens and other green vegetables and fruits contain complex B vitamins, which are essential for healthy hair growth. Bananas and chili peppers are also good sources of these nutrients.

- Broccoli, parsley, green peppers, and of course citrus fruits are just some of the many wonderful plants that contain high levels of vitamin C. This essential nutrient helps to improve blood flow to the scalp, which in turn supports healthy hair growth.

⮑ Vitamin E is essential for strong, healthy hair as well as for vigorous hair growth. Swiss chard, spinach, and other greens contain high levels of vitamin E, as do seeds and nuts. Nibbling on nuts and seeds throughout the day is a great way to boost vitamin E intake.

Green juices help improve the looks of your skin and nails fairly quickly, and they help you feel great almost instantly. Hair takes a long time to grow, so it may take a few months to a year of constant juicing for you to really notice a change in the way your hair looks, as well as in the way it feels.

Making green juices a central part of your daily intake is vital to successful hair growth, just as it is vital to repairing so many of the body's other tissues and organs. Think of it this way: Your problems with your hair probably did not begin overnight, and they are not going to be solved overnight, either. The average person's hair grows at a rate of approximately half an inch per month, although this does vary. So give your green juices time to work, and in the meantime, enjoy the many benefits they provide while you're waiting for your hair issues to resolve themselves.

Here are ten lovely recipes to help your body begin growing healthier hair. While any of the juices in this book are great for hair growth, these will help you to get started.

Ginger Greenie

5 kale leaves
1 medium cucumber
4 celery stalks, long fibers removed
2 medium yellow or green apples
1/2 lemon, peeled
½ inch ginger root, scrubbed and peeled

Wash all produce well, and then process in juicer.

Green Glory

1 handful spinach
2 kale leaves
1 large bunch parsley, rinsed well
1 large cucumber
2 celery stalks, long fibers removed

Wash all produce well, and then process in juicer.

Mighty Apple-Melon Juice

2 medium apples
2 cups cantaloupe chunks
2 cups honeydew melon chunks
6 kale leaves
6 Swiss chard leaves

Wash all produce well, and then process in juicer.

Royal Carrot Greenie

6 large carrots
1 small handful parsley, rinsed well
2 stalks asparagus (place in juicer bottom-first)
2 celery stalks, long fibers removed
2 small Brussels sprouts, halved

Wash all produce well, and then process in juicer.

Simple Pleasures Greenie

1 head Bibb or romaine lettuce
1 small handful spinach
2 medium apples or pears
1 lemon, peeled

Wash all produce well, and then process in juicer.

Fruity Spinach Blast

3 cups spinach
4 celery stalks, long fibers removed
1 medium cucumber
2 ripe grapefruits, peeled
1 lime, peeled
1 small green or yellow pear
1 mango, seeded and peeled
1 to 2 inches ginger root, scrubbed and peeled (optional)

Wash all produce well, and then process in juicer.

Cool Green Limeade

4 romaine lettuce leaves
2 cucumbers
4 celery stalks, long fibers removed
1 green apple, quartered
1 orange, peeled
3 limes, peeled
1/2 lemon, peeled

Wash all produce well, and then process in juicer. Fantastic over ice.

Triple-Fruit Greenie

1 handful parsley, rinsed well
3 kale leaves
2 medium carrots
2 celery stalks, long fibers removed
2 green or yellow apples
2 oranges, peeled
1 green or yellow pear

Wash all produce well, and then process in juicer.

Green Grape Goodness

4 kale leaves
1 medium cucumber
20 green seedless grapes
1 small green apple
1 lime, peeled (start with half, and add the other half if the flavor isn't too tart)

Wash all produce well, and then process in juicer.

Green Revival

1 handful spinach
1 small handful peppermint
1 small handful parsley, rinsed well
1 cucumber
3 lettuce leaves (Bibb or romaine work well)
4 celery stalks, long fibers removed
¼ lemon, peeled
½ inch ginger root, scrubbed and peeled

Wash all produce well, and then process in juicer.

Give Yourself an Energy Boost with Green Juice

Do you rely on coffee, soda pop, or candy for energy throughout the day? Do you stay up late, suffer from caffeine crashes or sugar crashes, and struggle to get up each morning? If you do, you're not alone. Many people rely on the quick chemical energy that caffeine and products containing processed sugar impart.

You now realize just how good green juices are for your body, and you have gained awareness about the way they provide you with perfect nutrition. You may be wondering how green juices provide such a powerful energy boost; after all, they are low in calories, they contain no caffeine, and they don't contain a lot of sugar.

- Nutrition – Proper nutrition leads to perfect, natural energy. Fruits and vegetables take in energy from the purest sources – water, sun, and soil – and they impart that energy to us in turn.

- Chlorophyll – Fresh plant foods are the best sources of this marvelous substance. Chlorophyll, by the way, is what gives green foods their green color. In the human body, it aids in proper oxygen transport, which in turn aids in the release of toxins and a dramatic increase in energy. To give yourself an even bigger chlorophyll boost, add blue green algae to your green juices. You'll be surprised at how rapidly your energy level improves.

- Detoxification – You learned a lot about detoxification in an earlier chapter, but did you know that detoxifying your system is one of the best ways to enjoy greater energy? You don't have to go on a juice fast to detox; just gradually eliminating toxins – or quitting them cold turkey if you can – and drinking at least two green juices daily will help you feel more energetic fast.

Digestion – Sluggish digestion leads to feelings of tiredness and general malaise. The fiber and enzymes green juices contain help to improve digestion. The standard American diet is full of foods that take a long time to move through the intestinal tract, and as they sit, they rot and leave toxins behind. Meat, cheese, and glutinous wheat products are just a few of the worst. Quitting them and moving toward a raw food diet that includes an abundance of green juices will speed up digestion, ensure you are properly nourished, and give you boundless energy for living life to its fullest.

Green juices are quick and easy to make. If you have not yet made your first juice, I encourage you to take a moment to do so now. Don't worry if you are missing certain ingredients – you'll discover that many fruits and vegetables are interchangeable with one another. Notice the way you feel before consuming your juice, drink it down, and wait for just a short time. You'll feel a wave of wonderful energy come over you. The more juice you drink, the better you'll feel.

It's understandable that changing the way you eat may take some time, but it's one of the best things you can do for yourself. Improved energy, and great health – what could be better? Here are ten delicious recipes to help you get the energy you need to make it through the day and enjoy a happier, healthier life.

Refreshing Apple Energy
2 apples, quartered
1 orange, peeled
1 lemon, peeled
1 handful spinach
1 kale leaf

Wash all produce well, and then process in juicer.

Celery-Apple Tonic
2 celery stalks, long fibers removed
1 green apple, quartered
1/2 small handful parsley, rinsed well
¼ lemon, peeled
1 inch section ginger root, scrubbed and peeled

Wash all produce well, and then process in juicer.

Salad Bar in a Glass

1 medium zucchini
3 medium tomatoes
2 carrots
1/4 sweet Vidalia onion
6 Swiss chard leaves
1 teaspoon olive oil (optional)
1 small pinch of sea salt (optional)
1 small pinch of black pepper (optional)
1 quick squeeze of lime or lemon (optional)

Wash all produce well, and then process in juicer. Stir in olive oil, salt, and pepper, then squeeze lemon or lime over top. Enjoy over ice.

Bunny's Delight

1 small head lettuce, your favorite type
6 medium carrots
2 celery stalks, long fibers removed

Wash all produce well, and then process in juicer.

Balancing Act Greenie

1 medium cucumber
4 kale leaves
1 large bunch cilantro, washed well
1 large apple, quartered
1 inch ginger root, scrubbed and peeled
1 lime, peeled (add a second lime if you want a tarter flavor)
3 celery stalks, long fibers removed

Wash all produce well, and then process in juicer.

Spinach Energy Shooter

3 handfuls spinach
1/4 lemon, peeled
1 tart green apple

Simple Energy

3 celery stalks, long fibers removed
1 small cucumber
2 kale leaves
2 Swiss chard leaves
1/2 bulb fennel
1 medium apple
1 medium pear
1 lemon, peeled
1 small handful parsley, rinsed well
1 small handful cilantro, rinsed well
½ inch section ginger root, or more to taste

Wash all produce well, and then process in juicer.

Kick-Starter Greenie

2 kale leaves
6 baby bok choi leaves
2 celery stalks, long fibers removed
1 small cucumber
1 medium carrot
1 large tomato
1/2 lemon, peeled
1/2 green apple
1 cup blueberries

Wash all produce well, and then process in juicer.

Veggie Magic

1 large bunch parsley, rinsed well
½ green apple (use the whole thing if you prefer a sweeter flavor)
2 medium carrots
4 celery stalks, long fibers removed

Wash all produce well, and then process in juicer.

Broccoli Blast

1 large stalk broccoli, including florets and stems

1 celery stalk, long fibers removed

2 medium carrots

2 oranges

1 green apple

1 lemon, peeled (If you'd like a tarter flavor and you have organic lemons, try leaving the peel on.)

Green Juices that Warm You Up

While you might be perfectly satisfied with cool juices most of the time, there are certain to be some times when you feel cold and want something that will warm you up. All too often, when hunger strikes and we're feeling cold, the first thing we reach for is a bit of our favorite comfort food – and that often comes with a heavy load of fat, salt, and maybe even added sugar.

It's true that a warm cup of soup does taste delicious, and it's fine to cook vegetables. But at the same time, it's important to recognize that heat kills the enzymes that provide you with the great feelings and energy green juices give you. Cooking vegetables oxidizes them, damages their cellular structure, and alters the way they nourish your body. Yes, cooked vegetables are definitely better for you than no vegetables at all, but cooking or even heating your fresh green juices is something you should never even consider trying.

So, what's a person to do when it's cold outside and you're faced with the prospect of drinking down a cold glass of green vegetable juice? The answer is a surprisingly simple one: Just add spice! There are a number of spices that will warm up your juices without actually heating them up and destroying the precious nutrients they contain. Some of these ingredients include:

- Ginger root – This tastes fantastic with many fruits and vegetables, and it creates a warm feeling in your stomach right after it is drunk. If you don't have fresh ginger root, you can use powdered ginger instead; mix the powder into your glass of juice after blending it. The flavor isn't quite so crisp and delicious, but warmth will be generated.

- Hot peppers – Jalapenos and habaneros are two examples of hot peppers that really heat up a juice blend. When dealing with hot peppers, there are a few precautions you should take. First consider wearing gloves when dealing with these peppers as they contain volatile oils that can cause discomfort. Second, always remove the seeds and white pith from the peppers before juicing them, unless you really want a fiery juice. Third, keep your face away from the juicer as you drop these peppers down the chute. I like to push them down with a large, watery vegetable such as a cucumber to keep the volatile components from becoming airborne and burning my eyes and sinuses.

- Powdered spices – Cayenne pepper, turmeric, and even cinnamon will add heat to your juices without physically warming them. To use these, simply create your juice recipe, and then mix the powdered spice into your glass. Be careful not to leave any lumps behind.

- Hot Sauces – Hot pepper sauces have complex flavors and they pack a lot of heat. They're easy to blend into fresh juices and they really do make your taste buds sing.

If you are not accustomed to hot, spicy foods, start out slowly. Reduce the amount of spice the following recipes call for by at least half, if not more. Taste the juice and add more spice if you like. Taste buds do change over time, and once you become accustomed to the flavors hot spices impart to juice recipes, you are likely to find yourself enjoying them very much and actually craving them.

Once you've got a good idea how spices will affect various juice blends, feel free to spice up any recipe in this book. In the meantime, here are ten wonderfully warming recipes to get you started.

Hot Tomato

1/4 cup purified water
2 ripe tomatoes
2 peeled cloves garlic
1 small handful spinach
2 medium carrots
1/4 sweet Vidalia onion
2 celery stalks, long fibers removed
¼ lemon, peeled
1-2 shakes hot sauce (more if you like it hot!)

Wash all produce well, and then process in juicer. Pour into a glass, then add hot sauce. Stir well and drink up.

Cozy Apple Ginger Juice

2 medium apples
6 leaves romaine lettuce
2 large carrots
1 inch section ginger root, scrubbed and peeled
1/4 lemon, peeled
¼ teaspoon powdered cinnamon

Wash all produce well, and then process in juicer. Add juice to glass, then add powdered cinnamon, Stir well and enjoy.

Lemon Ginger Soother

4 kale leaves
1 handful cilantro, rinsed well
2 small cucumbers
3 apples
3 celery stalks, long fibers removed
½ inch section ginger root, scrubbed and peeled
½ lemon, peeled

Wash all produce well, and then process in juicer.

Kale Hottie

2/3 teaspoon prepared horseradish
1 tablespoon low-sodium soy sauce
5 large ripe tomatoes
6 kale leaves
4 celery stalks, long fibers removed
2 lemons, peeled
1 dash hot sauce

Combine the horseradish and soy sauce in a glass. Wash all produce well, and then process in juicer. Add juice to glass, then add hot sauce. Stir well and add ice if desired.

Spicy Spinach Blend

1 handful spinach
1 small cucumber
2 celery stalks, long fibers removed
3 medium carrots
1/2 apple (use the whole apple if the juice tastes too bitter to you)
1 pinch turmeric

Wash all produce well, and then process in juicer. Pour into a glass, then blend powdered turmeric in before drinking. Feel free to add more spice if you enjoy the way it tastes.

Carrot-Ginger Soother

1 bunch cilantro, rinsed well
4 m carrots
1 medium apple
1/2 lemon, peeled
1 inch section ginger root, scrubbed and peeled

Wash all produce well, and then process in juicer.

Triple Green Apple Juice

2 stalks celery, long fibers removed
4 romaine lettuce leaves
2 small kale leaves
1 small handful spinach
1 large green apple (use two if the juice tastes overly bitter to you)
1/2 cucumber
1/2 lemon, peeled
½ inch section ginger root, scrubbed and peeled

Wash all produce well, and then process in juicer.

Spiced Pear Cider

4 romaine lettuce leaves
1 medium apple
2 medium pears
½ inch section ginger root, scrubbed and peeled
¼ teaspoon cinnamon

Wash all produce well, and then process in juicer.

Spinach with a Twist

    1 cup spinach
    2 large oranges
    ½ inch section ginger root, scrubbed and peeled

Wash all produce well, and then process in juicer.

Liquid Sunshine

    2 handfuls spinach
    2 cups fresh pineapple, cubed
    1 medium orange, peeled
    1 inch section ginger root, scrubbed and peeled

Wash all produce well, and then process in juicer.

Beat the Heat with Green Juices that Cool You Down

When it's hot outside, you might feel tempted to turn to a cold soda, a big glass of beer, or a giant helping of ice cream to cool down. The problem is that many traditional hot weather treats are far from good for you; for example, the caffeine in soda and the alcohol in beer both act as diuretics – instead of hydrating you so you stay cool, they dehydrate you and ultimately lead to greater discomfort. Keep consuming them over time, and you'll notice that you feel heavy, sluggish, and hot.

What you drink and eat really does make a difference in keeping your body temperature regulated, and luckily, green juices have the power to help you beat the heat, even when temperatures soar into the 100s. It's not just because juices are cool, though keeping them chilled and serving them over ice does help. There are some other reasons juices help you stay cool when the mercury rises.

On days when heat and humidity are high, the skin and muscles must compete for blood circulation. When temperatures outside are hot, the skin receives more blood as the body works hard to keep its temperature from becoming dangerously high. As a result, the muscles receive less blood, and lethargy results. Staying hydrated can help combat this, and certain green juices help to cool the body from the inside out. Some of the best ingredients to incorporate into juice recipes designed to cool you off include:

- Fruits and vegetables with high water content – melons, cucumbers, oranges and other citrus fruits are great choices. Mango, celery, and lettuce are also excellent for hydrating the body at a cellular level and helping it stay cool.

➲ Astringents – Anything that makes your mouth pucker is an astringent. Grapes, sour apples, and tart citrus like grapefruit are some examples of astringents. When you consume these foods, cells are encouraged to take up more water, which works to maintain a cooler core temperature.

➲ Leafy greens – Green leafy vegetables, as you know, are powerfully nutritious. They also contain calcium, which is a thermo regulator the body uses to keep internal temperature stable.

➲ Spicy seasonings – You might be surprised to see hot spices on a list of items that keep the body cool, but the fact that these foods promote sweating means they can be valuable in aiding with rapid cooling. It's vital that you stay hydrated when consuming hot spices, which is why they're the perfect match for other green juice ingredients.

Besides drinking plenty of fresh green juice during hot weather, pay attention to what else you are taking in. Keep drinking plenty of water, and be careful not to consume foods that are too salty, too sweet, or too high in fat. Keeping your system clean will help all the good nutrients within these juices to reach cells rapidly and do the work of cooling you off instead of being forced to act as detoxifiers.

You can use any of the recipes this book contains to help regulate your temperature during hot weather, however those that contain ingredients like the ones described above are most effective at keeping the body cool and comfortable. Following, you'll find ten delicious recipes that have been specifically designed to help you beat the heat.

Fresh Green Lemonade

> 10 leaves romaine lettuce
> 4 kale leaves
> 2 tart apples, quartered
> 1 lemon, peeled

Wash all produce well, and then process in juicer. Serve over ice.

Cool and Comfy

> 1 handful spinach
> 6 medium carrots
> 1 large cucumber

Wash all produce well, and then process in juicer. Serve over ice.

Cucumber-Cilantro Cooler

    2 large cucumbers
    10 leaves Romaine lettuce
    1 lemon, peeled
    5 leaves baby bok choi
    1 large handful cilantro, rinsed well
    1 celery stalk, long fibers removed
    1 inch section ginger root, scrubbed and peeled
    1/8 teaspoon cayenne pepper

Wash all produce well, and then process in juicer. Sprinkle cayenne over juice, then mix thoroughly. Serve over ice.

Lemon-Lime Cooler

    3 kale leaves
    2 handfuls spinach
    1 large cucumber
    1 large green apple
    ½ lime, peeled
    ½ lemon, peeled
    ½ inch section ginger root, scrubbed and peeled (optional – this recipe is nice with or without the ginger root.)

Wash all produce well, and then process in juicer. Serve over ice.

Kid-Friendly Greenie

    All water from 1 Thai coconut
    6 lettuce leaves, your choice
    3 medium green or yellow apples
    25 green grapes
    3 green or yellow pears
    1 cup fresh pineapple chunks

Wash all produce well, and then process in juicer. Serve over ice.

Cool Mint Limeade

1 head romaine lettuce
4 parsnips, peeled
4 large green apples
1 lime, peeled
2 large handfuls mint, rinsed well

Wash all produce well, and then process in juicer. Serve over ice. Garnish with additional lime or mint if desired.

Sweet and Spicy Limeade

4 cups spinach
3 inch section ginger root, scrubbed, peeled, and cut into 1-inch chunks
4 large apples
1/2 cup coconut water, chilled

Wash all produce well, and then process in juicer. Serve over ice.

How Sweet it Is

3 Bibb lettuce leaves
2 romaine lettuce leaves
1 small handful baby bok choi
10 baby carrots
1 sweet apple
1 orange or 2 tangerines

Wash all produce well, and then process in juicer. Serve over ice.

Easy Green Cooler

1 handful spinach
3 celery stalks, long fibers removed
6 romaine lettuce leaves
1 cucumber
2 large green pears, stems removed
¼ lemon, peeled

Wash all produce well, and then process in juicer. Serve over ice.

Green Melon Cooler

    3 kale leaves
    2 green apples
    2 cups honeydew melon
    ¼ lemon, peeled

Wash all produce well, and then process in juicer. Serve over ice.

Bonus Recipes

Use these wonderful recipes anytime you're looking for a simple, delicious green juice to enjoy on the spot. Make them, and the rest of the recipes in this book, your very own by substituting different fruits and vegetables for the ones listed. Enjoy!

Fresh and Green

2 cucumbers
4 celery stalks, long fibers removed
10 romaine lettuce leaves

Wash all produce well, and then process in juicer. Serve over ice.

Triple C-Monster

4 medium carrots
1 small handful collard greens
5 clementines, peeled

Wash all produce well, and then process in juicer. Serve over ice.

Super Citrus Greenie

2 tangerines, peeled
1 lemon, peeled
1 celery stalk, long fibers removed
1 small handful spinach
2 green or yellow apples

Wash all produce well, and then process in juicer. Serve over ice.

Glorious Morning

 1 cucumber
 2 celery stalks, long fibers removed
 1 large orange
 1 medium handful baby spinach
 1/2 yellow or green bell pepper
 3 kale leaves
 1 tomato
 2 medium carrots

Wash all produce well, and then process in juicer. Serve over ice.

Totally Green

 3 cucumbers
 2 parsnips
 3 green apples
 2 key limes, peeled
 4 celery stalks, long fibers removed
 4 handfuls spinach
 1 small handful cilantro, rinsed well

Wash all produce well, and then process in juicer. Serve over ice.

Hidden Greens Juice

 2 inch section ginger root, scrubbed, peeled, and cut into two pieces
 2 large oranges
 3 large apples
 3 ripe pears
 30 purple grapes
 2 big handfuls blueberries
 15 strawberries
 1 large cucumber
 6 kale leaves
 6 stalks celery, long fibers removed
 2 medium carrots

Wash all produce well, and then process in juicer. Serve over ice.

Sweet Mandarin Delight

  3 mandarins
  6 large strawberries
  1 tart apple
  2 cups baby carrots, peeled
  4 romaine lettuce leaves

Wash all produce well, and then process in juicer. Serve over ice.

Melon Dewdrop

  2 cups honeydew melon, in chunks or balls
  1 cucumber
  2 celery stalks
  2 cups baby lettuce leaves

Wash all produce well, and then process in juicer. Serve over ice.

Morning Energy Juice

  2 large yellow or green apples
  1 large carrot
  6 strawberries
  1 handful spinach or baby bok choi
  2 romaine lettuce leaves
  1 cup pineapple chunks
  1 lime, peeled (optional)

Wash all produce well, and then process in juicer. Serve over ice.

Sweet Pineapple-Kale Ale

  5 kale leaves
  ½ fresh pineapple, rind removed
  2 celery stalks, long fibers removed
  2 large carrots
  2 apples or pears
  1 inch section ginger root, scrubbed and peeled

Wash all produce well, and then process in juicer. Serve over ice.

Adding an Extra Kick to Your Green Juices: It's Easy!

Here you will learn how to add some interesting and easily available extra ingredients to your green juices and smoothies to make them even more amazing and nutrition-packed.

Let's get right to it - with some supplements you can add to your green juices to boost brainpower, heal the body and increase energy.

- Put some spice into your life with **cayenne pepper**. This is a wonderful supplement to add to your green juices. It does all kinds of good things for your organs including the brain. It also stops bleeding intestines, dissolves blood clots, increases circulation to the head to reduce the chances of aneurism or stroke. Just 1/8 of a teaspoon (of 1500,00 heat units) added to your green juices can help prevent Alzheimer's disease, and senility and improve mental clarity. Cayenne is actually *more* beneficial when done with green juicing since taking cayenne pepper alone can cause intense stomach cramps or digestive discomfort.

- Add some **algae** to your green juices. There are four major types of algae – spirulina, Chlorella, blue green algae, and Dunaliella (red algae). Most people in civilized nations consume way too much protein – and it is very hard for the body to break it down. What they really need are the amino acids in the proteins, and algae has a very high utilization percentage – which means your body can use up to 60-70% of it without having to work so hard to absorb it.

You can use just ½ teaspoon in your juices daily to get algae's great benefits. Algae powder is the best thing to add to your juices, and actually is preferable over taking algae tablets because they are harder to digest. Just one type of algae – the blue green variety is a known brain booster. It is rich in neuropeptide precursors. These are important for the neurotransmitters in the brain to communicate with one another. It makes for better learning and memory as well as improving our abilities to adapt to changes in our environment – otherwise known as stress! The improved functioning of these neuropeptides also means that your pineal gland, an important endocrine gland in the center of the brain functions better. Many call it the 'master' gland of the body.

⮑ Put a little **nutritional yeast** (*Saccharomyces cerevisiae*) in your green juices to prevent and aid: dementia, Alzheimer's disease, nervous system disorders, Multiple Sclerosis, premature senility, schizophrenia, Tourette's syndrome, neurological disorders, anxiety, depression, and emotional weakness. The reason nutritional yeast is such a great additive for your green juices is because it is full of B vitamins, which the nervous system and brain require to function at their best. One word of caution, however, if you have gout or the tendency to develop gout, don't use this supplement because the high protein levels can aggravate this disease. You can start with just two TBS per green juice – and add to just about every recipe presented in this guide.

⮑ **Barley or wheat grass** is a great addition to your green juices. Because of their incredibly high nutrient content, added with your leafy greens and highly alkalizing green vegetables, barley and wheat grass take your green juices to the next level – they are literally food for your brain, so you will feel energized, mentally clear and full of life every day. Just add a few freshly juiced greens if you have the right kind of juicer (just a shot glass full is sufficient to add to any green juice) or use a few tablespoons of wheat grass or barley powder if you aren't juicing fresh.

⮑ **Organic, unfiltered apple cider vinegar with the "mother"** is also a wonderful way to boost brainpower. It also removes calcium deposits form the body so it can treat joints and muscles too. It also balances the body's pH levels, which the brain requires for its best performance. You can start with just 1 tablespoon per green juice you consume and add more as you desire over time.

There are of course other supplement you can add to your green juices – super food powders, and herbs, just to name a few, but these are a few great ones to start with and they are often easily found at health food stores or your local market. Green juicing is already amazing on its own, but if you want the Ferrari of green juices – these supplements will take your juicing habit to the next level.

Getting Ready: How to Prepare Ingredients for the Best Green Juices

If you don't prep your vegetables and fruits properly, you can miss out on some of the benefits of green juicing. This chapter covers all you need to know to get it right from the start.

Here are some simple, general steps to make sure you get the most out of the fruits and vegetables that you juice:

- Use organics whenever possible.

- Wash all fruits and vegetables before cutting into them – even ones with skin you won't be consuming.

- Always cut larger fruits or vegetables if you are feeding them into a centrifugal force juicer so that they can be juiced completely.

- Roll leafy greens up into a cylindrical shape before adding to the juicer, and push them through with firmer ingredients to get the most out of them.

- Peel non-organic fruits and vegetables to remove any pesticide remaining.

Use the following list to make preparing a variety of fruits and vegetables easier than ever.

Apples – To prepare apples for juicing, cut them in quarters. While many people don't eat apple seeds, it's fine to leave them in place for juicing. They contain vitamin

B17, potassium, and magnesium, and they're high in protein. If you're using a blender to make your juice, it's best to remove the core and stem to avoid excess wear and tear on the blade.

Apricots – Wash the apricots and either tear them in half or slice them in half to access the pit, which should be removed before juicing.

Asparagus – Asparagus has delicate tops, so use care in washing this vegetable. Push asparagus into your juicer bottom end first.

Avocado – Avocados and juicers just don't mix. If you want to use an avocado in a recipe, juice other ingredients first, then add them to the blender, along with the avocado's flesh.

Bananas – Just like avocados, bananas don't do well in juicers. To thicken a recipe with banana, make your juice first, and then blend it together with the banana in the blender.

Basil – Wash carefully to remove any dirt or sand. Either juice leaves on their own or add stems, too; just roll these up and push them into the juicer with firmer produce.

Beets – Peel your beets under running water, and cut them in quarters before adding them to the juicer.

Bell Peppers – Remove the stems from bell peppers before juicing. Cut them in halves or quarters, and don't worry about removing the seeds. They're a nutritious addition to juice.

Blackberries – Do not wash blackberries until right before using them – washing ahead of time hastens spoilage. Simply rinse in a strainer, and be sure to pick out any thorny stems before juicing.

Blueberries – Like other berries, blueberries shouldn't be washed until just before use. To clean blueberries, simply rinse them in a sieve.

Broccoli – Slice any discolored florets, leaves, or stem parts off broccoli after washing. You can add the whole plant – stems, stalks, and florets – to juices.

Butter Lettuce – Tear leaves from stalk and rinse individually. To add to juices, just roll the leaves together into a cylindrical shape, then push down the juicer's chute.

Cabbage – Either tear off individual leaves or cut sections of cabbage that will easily fit into the juicer's chute.

Cactus Pears – Peel carefully. Cut down to size after peeling if needed.

Cantaloupe – Cut in half, and then scoop out seeds. Cut each half into four sections, and then cut each section into chunks after removing the rind. If you have a melon baller, you can simply scoop chunks from each half of the cantaloupe – put these into a bowl or measuring cup to preserve as much juice as possible.

Carrots – Just wash carrots thoroughly and push them down the juicer's chute. If they're not organic, you'll need to peel them, as well.

Celery Root (Celeriac) – Scrub with a brush to remove any hidden dirt. Peel to prevent an overly earthy flavor if you like; cut this heavy root into quarters to make juicing easier on your machine.

Celery – Remove any really heavy fibers from celery stalks before juicing. After rinsing, simply push through the chute, tops and all.

Chard – Rinse leaves carefully, then roll together and push through the juicer's chute. Chard is often grown in sandy soil, so be sure to use extra care in cleaning this leafy green!

Cherries – After washing, use a cherry pitter or a small paring knife to remove the hard pits before juicing.

Chayotes – After washing, cut down to size, and then push through the juicer's chute.

Cilantro – Cilantro is usually grown in sandy soil and it can retain a lot of sand. Fill a bowl with water, submerge the cilantro, and swish it around to remove the majority of the sand, and then give it a final rinse. Roll up into a ball before adding to your juicer.

Collard Greens – Wash carefully and roll together into a cylindrical shape before pushing into the chute.

Cranberries – Simply rinse and add to juicer.

Cucumbers – If you have a waxed cucumber or one that isn't organic, you'll need to peel it before adding it to the juicer. Otherwise, simply rinse and push down the chute.

Dandelion – Only use dandelion greens harvested from areas where no chemicals are used. Wash the leaves and roll up to add to the juicer.

Dill – Rinse well and add the fronds to your juicer. I like to put them in at the same time as other greens, which I then push through with a cucumber for a nice light drink.

Eggplant – Eggplant is quite bitter and doesn't lend itself well to juicing as it has a firm, spongy texture. This vegetable is one that I don't use for juice.

Fennel – Cut into quarters after rinsing, then put through the juicer. You can juice the tops as well as the bulbs.

Garlic – Try a little at a time and be sure to peel before juicing. Garlic is great with tomatoes, basil, and cucumbers.

Ginger Root – Cut or snap a section off the main ginger root, then scrub it well. Scrape the peel off and add the root to the juicer.

Grapefruit – Peel the zest off with a peeler, retaining as much white pith as possible, since it contains nutrients that help you absorb vitamin C. Cut into quarters or chunks before juicing if it won't fit down the chute whole.

Grapes – Wash grapes, and then remove stems. If grapes contain seeds, don't worry – just add them to the juicer whole.

Jalapeno- Wash, remove top, and cut in half. Remove the pith and seeds before juicing, and be careful not to rub your eyes afterward. A little jalapeno in your juice will help clear a stuffy nose; I find it is also helpful in eliminating headaches.

Jicama – Don't peel jicama before juicing since there are loads of nutrients in and near the skin. Simply slice into large chunks to make the task of juicing easier on your machine.

Kale – Wash carefully, then roll leaves together into a cylindrical shape before shoving down the chute.

Kiwis – Kiwifruit should be peeled before juicing; once you've got the peel off, just drop the whole kiwi into the juicer.

Leeks – Slice in half lengthwise, then rinse between each layer. Leeks are grown in sandy soil, so be sure to clean carefully. The root and green leaves are fine to add to your juice.

Lemons – Peel zest away from pith using vegetable peeler, or if you really love the flavor of lemon and have organic lemons, simply slice in half after rinsing and add to the juicer, peel and all.

Limes – Follow the same procedure as you would for lemons, retaining white pith and seeds. Lime zest can be quite bitter so use caution about adding entire limes to your juice unless this is a flavor you enjoy.

Mangos – Cut away from flat, central seed, then cut into spears or chunks. Mango skin is fine to add to the juicer, but it will contribute a slightly bitter flavor so keep this in mind when preparing this fruit.

Melons – Cut in half and scoop out seeds. Next, either use a melon baller to scoop fruit into a bowl, or cut each half into sections, peel, and drop chunks into a bowl before juicing.

Mint – Wash well, then roll into a ball before juicing. Like other greens, it's best to push mint through the juicer with a firm ingredient like melon or cucumber.

Mustard Greens – Use mustard greens sparingly as they have an intense flavor. Rinse and roll up before adding to juicer with other savory ingredients.

Onions – Remove papery outer skin, and then cut into sections before juicing. The same procedure should be followed for garlic if you choose to use it in savory juice recipes. For green onions, simply rinse well and remove roots, then add to the juicer, green tops and all.

Papaya – Papayas should be cut in half and skinned before being added to your juicer. The seeds are very high in protein and can be added to juices with no adverse side effects.

Parsley – Parsley is normally grown in sandy soil, so it has a tendency to be gritty. Fill a big bowl with water and swish the parsley around to remove sand and dirt, then give it a final rinse. Simply roll it into a ball and add it to your juicer.

Parsnips – These nutty, slightly spicy, slightly sweet root vegetables should be treated like carrots. Just wash the well and add them to your juicer. Peel them first if they're not organic.

Peaches – Cut in half, then remove pit. Add to juicer, fuzzy skin and all.

Pears – Remove stems and cut into halves or quarters before adding to the juicer.

Pineapple – Cut into quarters, and then cut spiny skin away from fruit. Section into spears and add to juice. If the core is woody, remove it; if not, add it to the juicer.

Plums – Slice in half, remove pit, and add to juicer.

Pomegranates – Fill a large bowl with water. Slice the pomegranate in half without pulling the two halves away from one another. Submerge it into the bowl and tear apart, breaking it up into chunks. The seeds will sink and the white pith will float; skim the pith away with a slotted spoon or spatula, then pour the water into a strainer to get to the seeds, which can then be dropped into the juicer. Don't worry if a little white pith remains; it will simply end up in the pulp to be discarded.

Radishes – Like other root vegetables, these can simply be rinsed and added to juice. Skin if not organic, and think twice about using the leaves as they can be very spicy.

Raspberries – As with other berries, wait to wash until just before juicing. Simply rinse in a strainer and be sure to remove any thorny stems or berry caps that might remain.

Romaine Lettuce – Tear individual leaves from the stalk, rinse carefully to remove any sand or dirt, and roll together into a cylinder before adding to juicer.

Scallions – Simply rinse and juice. Add to the juicer root end first.

Spinach - Separate leaves from roots, then wash well to remove any sand. Roll leaves into a ball, and then add to juicer.

Squash – For winter squash, including pumpkins, cut in half, then scoop out seeds. Add these to your juice, as they contain anti-cancer agents. Cut into large chunks after peeling skin. For summer squash, simply cut into large chunks and add to juicer.

Strawberries – Rinse and add to the juicer whole. You can leave the tops on if you like, or cut them off.

Sugar Snap Peas – Simply rinse and run through the juicer, pods and all.

Sweet Potatoes – Scrub thoroughly and cut into large chunks.

Tangerines – As with other citrus fruits, simply remove the zest with a vegetable peeler, leaving the nutritious pith intact. Drop whole into the juicer, or cut in half to fit the chute. If you have organic tangerines and you love the taste of their zest, try leaving all or part of the zest intact to add nutrients and an interesting flavor to your juice.

Tarragon – These tiny leaves are wonderfully flavorful; tear them off their woody stems before adding to the juicer. I like to moisten a firm, juicy fruit or vegetable and roll it around in the tarragon leaves so they stick to it; that way I get as much tarragon flavor as possible into my juice.

Tomatoes – Tomatoes are very easy to work with; just remove the stems, wash well, and add to the juicer whole. If you have very large tomatoes, cut them down to size before pushing them down the chute.

Turnips – Scrub well and cut into chunks before adding to juicer. Although some turnips are small enough to juice whole, they are very hard and can be tough for a juicer to handle and could cause damage if left intact.

Watermelon – Just wash your watermelon, then cut it in half. Use a scoop or spoon to remove the flesh, which you'll want to put into a measuring cup or bowl before adding to juicer. Don't worry about the seeds – they can go right into the juicer without causing any problems, and they'll add a bit of extra protein and minerals to your juice.

Wheatgrass- Rinse and roll into a ball. Now, push it through at the same time with a juicy, firm ingredient like a pear or a cucumber. Most juicers can handle small amounts of wheatgrass when juiced this way, but don't try to add a lot of wheatgrass on its own unless your juicer is designed specifically to extract the juice from it.

Zucchini – Scrub zucchinis well before juicing, and simply cut the tough stem end off. A zucchini makes a great mild-tasting addition to any green juice!

Taking Your Juices to the Next Level with Super Foods

Perhaps you've heard of goji berries or acai, and you may have heard about maca root powder. If you think you've never heard of cacao, think again; this powerful super food is what gives chocolate its enticing flavor! In this chapter, you'll learn about many super foods you can add to your juices and blends to kick your body into stratospheric levels of health and wellness, plus you'll learn more about why some really common fruits and vegetables are considered to be super foods.

Super Foods are so named because of their high nutrient content, and because they contain important phytochemicals that are capable of increasing health and wellbeing. Many super foods have already made their way onto our lists: Spinach, blueberries, beets, and sweet potatoes are just a few examples of common super foods. Besides these more common ones, there are hundreds of others, which can be added to your green juices. To get the best benefits, look for super foods with high ORAC values.

What is an ORAC Value?

ORAC is an acronym that stands for *Oxygen radical Absorbance Capacity*. In a nutshell, an ORAC value is a way to measure a food's level of antioxidants. Foods that rank higher on the ORAC scale have high levels of antioxidants, so these foods are best for neutralizing the free radicals that can harm the body at a cellular level. Eating plenty of super foods with high ORAC values is an excellent way to help keep you looking and feeling youthful while eliminating damage that contributes to disease and age-related degenerative processes. Health experts recommend that people consume at least 3,000 to 5,000 ORAC units daily; without juicing, you can see how that might be a stretch when the downfalls of the modern diet are considered.

The Health Benefits of Super Foods

The health benefits of super foods are numerous. Eating plenty of these foods on a regular basis – and drinking them in your juice – can do more than simply protect you from rapid aging. Here are some ways adding super foods to your diet will benefit your health:

- ⮑ Super foods reduce the risk of chronic disease developing
- ⮑ Eating super foods as a major part of the diet may prolong healthy lifespan
- ⮑ People who consume lots of super foods are generally less prone to obesity than those who do not

Top Ten Common Superfoods for Juicing

Ten top superfoods to consider include the following. The ORAC values listed are for 100 grams of the food, which comes out to about 3.5 ounces.

1. **Beets** – These vibrant root vegetables are known to help decrease hypertension, which is just one reason to include them in your green juices. They also contain loads of vitamins and minerals, and they have an ORAC score of 841.

2. **Blueberries** – With an ORAC value of 2,400. Blueberries are powerful as well as tasty. They contain antioxidants that may reduce the risk of cancer.

3. **Blackberries** – These delicious berries contain lots of fiber, vitamins, minerals, and antioxidants. They come in just behind blueberries with an ORAC value of 2,036.

4. **Broccoli** – When your mother urged you to eat lots of broccoli, I hope you listened! This super food contains an abundance of vitamins and minerals; in addition, it has an ORAC value of 890.

5. **Kale** – In case you're wondering why kale is such a popular ingredient in green juices, it's not just because this leafy green is wonderfully nutritious in

a variety of ways. Kale is the most powerful green in another way: It has an ORAC value of 1,770.

6. **Raspberries** – Raspberries are wonderfully flavorful, and they contain loads of vitamins as well as plenty of heart-healthy fiber. Raspberries have an ORAC value of 1,220.

7. **Red Bell Pepper** – Not too sweet, and very light tasting, red bell pepper contains high levels of vitamin C as well as lots of vitamin A. It is also filled with antioxidants, which give it an ORAC score of 713.

8. **Spinach** – If you prefer the taste of spinach over the flavor of kale, don't worry. Spinach is great for you, and it scores high with an ORAC value of 1,260.

9. **Strawberries** – Red, ripe, strawberries have an ORAC value of 1,540. They also contain lots of vitamin C and fiber, plus they're a low-calorie choice with plenty of flavor to add to green juices.

10. **Tomatoes** – Ripe, red tomatoes contain lycopene, which is an antioxidant that is less abundant in other foods. They also contain plenty of fiber, potassium, and vitamin C. Tomatoes have an ORAC value of 189. The more you enjoy, the higher that number will be.

Super Food Supplements

Not only can you enjoy everyday fruits and vegetables and benefit from their superb nutrition, you can also add a powerful antioxidant boost to green juices while adding exceptional flavor, just by stirring in a small amount of one of these supplements. Here's a list of 15 outstanding super food supplements and their approximate ORAC value per 100 grams (the oxygen free radical absorption capacity):

Food	ORAC Value
1. Sumac	312,400
2. Ground Cloves	290,283
3. Sorghum Bran	240,000

4. Dried Oregano	175,295
5. Dried Rosemary	165,280
6. Dried Thyme	157,290
7. Ground Cinnamon	131,420
8. Ground Turmeric	127,068
9. Dried & Ground Vanilla	122,400
10. Ground Sage	119,200
11. Szechuan Peppers	118,500
12. Acai Powder	102,700
13. Maca Root Powder	90,500
14. Cocoa Powder	55,653
15. Fresh Thyme	27,426

Adding Superfoods to Green Juices

As you can see, most of these superfoods are powders and as such, they don't contain any juice. Each of these superfoods also has a distinct flavor; for example, cocoa powder provides a taste of chocolate, while dried, ground vanilla provides the famous vanilla flavor so many people love. Szechuan peppers are very spicy, while many other super-foods; including thyme, sage, and oregano have distinctive herbal flavors.

If you'd like to add one or more of these ingredients to a green juice, the best way to do it is to prepare the juice first, pour it into a glass, then sprinkle the super food onto it. Some other super foods you can add this way include spirulina, kelp, and even certain essential oils, all of which add flavor and potent nutritional power to the juice you're drinking.

If you decide you want to try adding some essential oils to your juices, you'll love the flavor they add, and your body will appreciate the powerful healing boost they provide.

Here are a few of the best essential oils you can add to finished juices, along with their ORAC values:

- **Clove Essential Oil** – This is powerful stuff. It adds a hot, spicy, slightly sweet flavor to juices (try it with apple, pears, and spinach!) plus it has the biggest ORAC number or any essential oil: 1,078,700. Use just one drop at a time and be sure you're getting pure therapeutic grade essential oil to reap the benefits.

- **Peppermint Essential Oil** – Not only does peppermint essential oil help to freshen the breath, it also helps keep appetite in check while increasing mental clarity and promoting alertness. Peppermint essential oil has an ORAC value of 137,300.

- **Lemon Essential Oil** – When fresh lemons are hard to come by and you want to add a nutritional boost plus a zippy flavor to your juice, try a drop of lemon essential oil. Its ORAC value is 660.

These are just a few of the many essential oils that are suitable for ingestion. When using them in juices, just add between one and two drops to the juice in your glass. Each drop contains the essence of a huge amount of the plant it is made with; for example, it takes 28 cups of mint to make one drop of peppermint essential oil.

Your Super Encyclopedia Of Greens

In this chapter you will enjoy an alphabetized master list of greens, fruits, vegetables, and even additional mix-ins that can add some wonderfully surprising health benefits to your body. Think of this chapter as your encyclopedia of green juicing. You'll end up knowing all the health benefits of each ingredient as well as how they taste, what exactly is in them, and why they work, whether they are a protein, vitamin, mineral or other compound which is really great for your body. You'll also learn about possible side effects (though they are minimal) and any ingredients you should avoid, and why.

You can use this section of the guide as a reference while you are learning to make your own green juices, and over time, you will probably become a green juicing aficionado, knowing which things to juice when and why, without having to even look at these pages!

Name of Green	Health Benefits	Vitamins Minerals Nutrients	Taste	Possible Side Effects
Alfalfa	Used by the Chinese since the 6th century to aid numerous ailments, it cures kidney problems, reduces fluid retention and swelling, supports glandular functioning, lowers cholesterol levels, prevents strokes, relieves auto-immune disorders, cleanses the blood, bowels and liver, nourishes the digestive system and is one of the best land-based sources of trace minerals. In Arabic, it is called the 'Father of Plants" since its roots go deep into the earth to draw up nutrients form the soil.	B1, B6, C, E, K, trace minerals calcium, magnesium, phosphorous, iron, potassium	Earthy and moist	As with any herbal remedy, you have to be careful not to overdo it. If too much Alfalfa is consumed, the red blood cells will break down, and an amino acid called *canavanine* can aggravate a disease called Lupus. This amino acid is usually only found in the seeds and sprouts, though not the mature leaves. This plant should be avoided if you are pregnant because *canavanine* can also disrupt hormonal cycles.

Name of Green	Health Benefits	Vitamins Minerals Nutrients	Taste	Possible Side Effects
Arugula also known as rocket, roquette, arugula and rucola.	Arugula is an aromatic salad green. It is a cruciferous vegetable. Cruciferous vegetables are associated with reduced risk of cancer in many studies. Arugula is rich with valuable antioxidants, considered essential in preventing free radical activity in the body. Studies show that vitamin A and flavonoid compounds in arugula may help protect the body from skin cancer, lung cancer and oral cancer. Arugula is also a rich source of phytochemicals like sulforaphane, which has excellent chemo protective effects and helps to fight carcinogens. Furthermore, Arugula is a good source of carotenoids, fat-soluble pigments that are known to help prevent macular degeneration. The vitamin C in arugula may help in the prevention of cataracts but it is also a powerful antioxidant that helps prevent cancer, boosts the immune system and fights the common cold. Vitamin A is a powerful antioxidant, boosts immunity and is great for the eyes, skin, bones and teeth. Arugula also provides 100% of the daily need for vitamin K with just three cups. Vitamin K is known to promote bone health and brain function while acting as an anti-inflammatory and antioxidant. Arugula supports weight loss. Due to its extremely low calorie content, while being packed with nutrients. Arugula supports bone health with low oxalate levels, and high vitamin K levels. Additionally, calcium, potassium, magnesium, manganese and vitamin C are all considered good contributors to positive bone health.	C, K and A. In addition to fighting free radical activity, these vitamins offer great immune system support. Arugula is also a good source of calcium, iron, potassium, manganese and phosphorous, all essential minerals. ***Low in Oxalate*** Oxalates inhibit mineral absorption in the body. Other healthy leafy greens, such as spinach, have high levels of oxalate. However, arugula appears to offer relatively low levels of oxalate, making it a healthier alternative for people seeking foods high in calcium and other essential minerals.	Tangy, Zesty	Arugula has no side effects

Name of Green	Health Benefits	Vitamins Minerals Nutrients	Taste	Possible Side Effects
Basil	Basil, a popular herb is used around the world. In addition to its versatile flavor, basil offers many health benefits. One of the primary medicinal uses for basil is for its anti-inflammatory properties. This effect stems from eugenol, a volatile oil in basil that blocks enzymes in the body that cause swelling, making basil an ideal treatment for people with arthritis. Basil, especially as an extract or oil, is known to have exceptionally powerful antioxidant properties that can arm the body against premature aging, common skin issues, age-related problems and even some types of cancer. Basil is also full of flavonoids orientin and vicenin, plant pigments that shield your cell structures from oxygen and radiation damage. Both fresh basil and basil oil have strong antibacterial capabilities. In fact, basil has proven to stop the growth of many bacteria, even those resistant to other antibiotics. Basil can be applied to wounds to help prevent bacterial infections. Also, by adding basil oil to your salad dressings, you can help ensure your vegetables are safe to eat. Basil oil can be used to treat constipation, stomach cramps and indigestion as well as the cold, flu, asthma, whooping cough, bronchitis and sinus infections. It is also a great source of magnesium, an essential mineral that helps the body's blood vessels relax, which can improve blood flow.	A, C, K, dietary fiber, manganese, magnesium, potassium	A fresh basil leaf eaten directly from the plant has an initial subtle peppery flavor. It then evolves into a slightly sweet flavor with a delicate menthol aroma.	There are no side effects for basil.

Name of Green	Health Benefits	Vitamins Minerals Nutrients	Taste	Possible Side Effects
Beet Greens & Stems	Because beet greens and stems are high in vitamin C, providing 30% of your total daily allowance in one serving, they act as a coenzyme to help synthesize certain amino acids. Due to high vitamin C levels, they also help the body produce collagen, a protein that supports healthy skin, bones, teeth and blood vessels. Your immune system also needs vitamin C to make white blood cells, which fight off infections. About 90 percent of vitamin C in the American diet comes from fruits and vegetables, such as beet greens. According to Nellie Hedstrom, nutrition specialist for the University of Maine Extension service. Your body uses fat to process and store vitamin A, which remains in your system longer than water-soluble vitamins. Vitamin A is necessary for good vision, playing a role in light absorption in the rods and cones of your retina. You also need vitamin A for cell differentiation, immunity and healthy skin. *Folate -* Beet greens provide small levels of folate -- about 2 1/2 percent of your daily value. Higher levels of folate exist in the bulb, about 17 percent of your daily value, so eat the whole plant, if possible. Folate functions in DNA synthesis, so has many important roles in your body such as preventing birth defects, making healthy blood cells and fighting cancer and heart disease. Folate is most well known for preventing spinal defects in developing babies, and is therefore a vital nutrient for pregnant women.	Vitamins A, C, K, B6, E (Alpha Tocopherol), low in Saturated Fat and Cholesterol. High in Protein, Folate, Iron, Zinc, Pantothenic Acid, Phosphorus and a great source of Dietary Fiber, Thiamin, Riboflavin, Calcium, Magnesium, Potassium, Copper and Manganese.	Earthy and Bitter	Beet Greens and stems have no side effects, but they may cause stomach upset due to their bitterness if not used in moderation.

Name of Green	Health Benefits	Vitamins Minerals Nutrients	Taste	Possible Side Effects
Bok Choy	Bok Choy is a type of Chinese cabbage that doesn't look like a typical cabbage. It has dark green leaves connected to white stalks. One cup has just 9 calories and barely a trace of fat, yet delivers protein, dietary fiber and almost all the essential vitamins and minerals. Bok Choy is a nutrient-dense food that offers several health benefits. It is also very low in calories.	Vitamins C, K, A, B-complex, antioxidants that are indicative of the Brassica family of plants - thiocyanates, indole-3-carbinol, lutein, zeaxanthin, sulforaphane and isothiocyanates, moderate source of minerals like calcium, phosphorous, potassium, manganese, iron and magnesium	Tastes like a cross between cabbage and lettuce, or perhaps spinach with a slight nutty flavor	There are no side effects to eating bok Choy
Broccoli Leaves and Flowers	Used by the Romans, broccoli is considered a super-food due to its many nutrients. It is often called the crown jewel of nutrients. The US didn't cultivate broccoli until the 20th century but it was used long before that. Broccoli originated in Asia minor. Roman farmers called it 'the five green fingers of Jupiter.' It prevents cancer, maintains a healthy nervous system, regulates blood sugar levels, reduces cholesterol and helps with digestion due to its fiber content. Its high content of vitamin A is good for maintaining eyesight. Thanks to glucoraphanin, it also helps to repair skin cells.	A Brassica vegetable, it contains special antioxidants that occur specifically in this plant family: thiocyanates, indole-3-carbinol, lutein, zeaxanthin, sulforaphane and isothiocyanates, also Vitamins, A, B5, B1, B6, K, E, C, folic acid, fiber and calcium, iron, magnesium, potassium, manganese, and dietary fiber.	Tastes mild and earthy.	For those who are taking blood-thinning medications, the excessive intake of broccoli is not a wise choice since it may interfere with the medications, thereby increasing the risk of stroke. Eating over one to two cups of broccoli a day may also increase the chances of dealing with kidney stones, so broccoli should be used sparingly in green juices.

Name of Green	Health Benefits	Vitamins Minerals Nutrients	Taste	Possible Side Effects
Endive, also known as Escarole	Endive is closely related to chicory. It is a cool-season crop native to Asia minor. It has curly narrow leaves as well as broad leaves. Current research studies suggest that high inulin and fiber content in escarole help reduce glucose and LDL cholesterol levels in diabetes and obese patients. It also helps to maintain healthy mucus membranes and skin. Its high content of vitamin A is good for maintaining eyesight.	Vitamins C, A, Beta Carotene, B-complex vitamins (B1, B3, B5, B6) good source of minerals like manganese, copper, iron, and potassium. Manganese is used as a co-factor for the antioxidant enzyme, *superoxide dismutase.* Potassium is an important intracellular electrolyte helps counter the hypertension effects of sodium.	Tangy and bittersweet taste.	Although this green leafy vegetable contains high concentrations of bitter glycosides and inulin, there are no known side effects when this vegetable is eaten in moderation.
Chard, also known as Swiss Chard	Swiss chard is packed full of good stuff. Recent research has shown that chard leaves contain at least 13 different polyphenol antioxidants, including kaempferol, the cardio protective flavonoid that's also found in foods like broccoli and kale. It is also full of syringic acid, which is known for regulating blood sugar. It is a special flavanoid that is known to inhibit activity of an enzyme called alpha-glucosidase, which means fewer carbohydrates that we consume are broken down into simple sugars. This means a lesser incident of blood sugar related illnesses like Diabetes. Chard also contains a beet-like phytonutrients called betalain, which help with inflammation and free radical absorption. Chard also helps to support bone health with some of the highest levels of vitamin K - an amazing 716% DV is only exceeded by kale, spinach, and collard greens. Since it is full of iodine, chard also protects the thyroid.	Vitamins K1, A, C, E, B1, B2, B3, B5, B6, tryptophan, magnesium, potassium, iron, manganese, copper, choline, calcium, phosphorous, folate, zinc, bioton, high iodine content	Strong, earthy taste	There are no known side effects of eating Swiss Chard, however, if you have an over-active thyroid, consult a doctor before consuming large quantities.

Name of Green	Health Benefits	Vitamins Minerals Nutrients	Taste	Possible Side Effects
Chickweed	A low-growing, soft plant often mistaken as a common weed. The whole plant is used to treat cuts, and also to relieve itching caused by eczema and psoriasis. It is also known to be good for rheumatism. It is demulcent (forms a soothing film over a mucous membrane, relieving minor pain and inflammation of the membrane). Mild alterative that corrects overall body imbalances. Taken internally, it helps soothe inflammation in the urinary system (eg. mild bladder infections, gastric and peptic ulcers). It also a good blood purifier by carrying away toxins. Internal use may also help to treat bronchitis, arthritis, and cold symptoms.	Rich in vitamin C, beta carotene, Vitamins B1, B2, and B3, Bio-flavonoids (including glycoside rutin) Coumarins, Omega 6 fatty acids, and trace minerals like copper, calcium, magnesium, manganese, iron, and silicon	Earthy, slightly bitter taste	No adverse effects.
Cilantro	One of the best benefits of cilantro is that it binds to heavy metal sin the body to help expel them as toxins. It has been used by naturopaths for centuries and was even considered a curative in Greek and Roman times. Cilantro reveres adverse effects of cardiovascular disease, can help cure diabetes, has anti-anxiety properties to calm your mood, improves sleep, lowers blood sugar levels, and has antibacterial, antifungal and antioxidant properties. Cilantro can also help lower 'bad' cholesterol. It has been used in Ayurvedic and Chinese medicine and is also a curative for poor digestion.	Rich in thiamin, zinc, dietary fiber and vitamins A, C, E and K. It has trace amounts of riboflavin, niacin, vitamin B6, folate, pantothenic acid, calcium, iron, magnesium, phosphorous, potassium, copper and manganese	Some call it 'soapy' in taste, but it is more like a mild mint or fresh tasting green	No known adverse effects of cilantro
Collard Greens	Collard greens help to improve bile production in the liver, lower bad cholesterol, offers a cancer-preventative in the form of 4 specific glucosinolates found in this cruciferous vegetable: glucoraphanin, sinigrin, gluconasturtiian, and glucotropaeolin. Collard greens help with overall detoxification of the body and have an anti-inflammatory effect as well. Collards are also very low in calories so they are a great green to add to juices if you are watching your weight.	Full of vitamins A, C, K, B1, B2, B3 B6, E, manganese, fiber, calcium, choline, tryptophan, iron, magnesium, folate, Omega 3s, potassium, and phosphorous	Strong, sometimes bitter and earthy taste	Aside from drinking too much too soon to cause a 'healing crisis' collard greens have no other adverse effects

Name of Green	Health Benefits	Vitamins Minerals Nutrients	Taste	Possible Side Effects
Dandelion Greens	Low in calories, dandelion greens have been shown to improve skin, hair and nails, reverse certain cancers, and greatly detox the body. The best part is you can often pick them from your own back yard since they grow as a common weed. They also contain more protein per serving than spinach, and dandelion greens contain all the essential amino acids, so it is a complete plant protein.	High in vitamins C, A and beta-carotene, also full of calcium and iron, copper manganese, phosphorus, potassium, and magnesium. Dandelion greens also contain more calcium than kale.	Mild earthy taste	No known adverse effects
Dill	Native to Russia, the Mediterranean, and parts of Africa originally, this is a commonly grown herb all over the world now. Dill has two types of healing components: *monoterpenes*, including carvone, limonene, and anethofuran; and *flavonoids*, including kaempferol and vicenin. Dill also contains what are called 'volatile oils' (eugenol) act as a "chemo protective" food (much like parsley) to help neutralize particular types of carcinogens, such as the *benzopyrenes* that are in cigarette smoke, charcoal grill smoke, and the smoke produced by trash incinerators. Dill helps to prevent bone loss, since it is full of calcium and important trace minerals that help the body absorb that mineral. Dill has the ability prevent bad bacteria from growing in the body through its high levels of antioxidants.	Dill is full of folic acid, riboflavin, niacin, vitamin A, C, beta carotene, and trace minerals like copper, potassium, calcium, manganese, iron, and magnesium	Soft, sweet taste	No known adverse effects

Name of Green	Health Benefits	Vitamins Minerals Nutrients	Taste	Possible Side Effects
Fennel	Fennel belongs to the *Umbellifereae* family and is therefore closely related to parsley, carrots, dill and coriander. Fennel has a unique combination of phytonutrients—including the flavonoids *rutin*, *quercitin*, and various *kaempferol glycosides*—that give it strong antioxidant powers. It also contains a 'volatile oil' called anethole, which has been known to cure certain cancers. It does this by shutting down intercellular signaling system called *tumor necrosis factor* (or *TNF*)-*mediated signaling*. Fennel also protects the colon, the heart and the overall health of the body. It can lower blood pressure and reduce free radicals in the body.	Vitamins C, some B3, folate, fiber, potassium, manganese, molybdenum, phosphorous, calcium, iron, copper, magnesium, phytonutrients	Crunchy and slightly sweet	No known adverse effects
Kale	Kale is low in calories and has no fat so it is the perfect food if you are reducing your calories. Kale supports cardiovascular health, prevents lung and oral cancers, it prevents bone loss, and it also helps to detox the body due to high sulfur content.	More iron than beef, high in Vitamin K, A, C (ten times more than spinach), antioxidants, flavonoids, carotenoids, Omega 3s, calcium, fiber, sulfur	Often bitter due to high iron content, but you can't taste it in green juices	No known adverse effects
Miner's Lettuce	Sometimes confused with Purslane, Miner's Lettuce is picked from a trailing vine, and has tender, soft leaves. It has flourished in the wild for hundreds of years. Gold miner's used to eat it during the gold rush to keep their energy up. It grows all over California, but is also cultivated elsewhere.	Ascorbic acid (Vitamin C), A, iron, beta carotene, protein	Mild tasting	No known adverse effects
Mint	There are lots of varieties of mint. It was used traditionally in Indian and the Middle East and Asia. It is considered an aromatic. Mint soothes the digestive tract, and helps with a stomachache, as well as irritated bowel syndrome (IBS). It can help with skin disorders including acne, and helps to eliminate toxins from the body. Mint can also help to whiten the teeth and it also cleans the blood.	Rich in vitamin C and beta carotenes, also full of a good source of several essential minerals, including magnesium, copper, iron, potassium, and calcium	Sweet with a cool aftertaste	No known adverse effects

Name of Green	Health Benefits	Vitamins Minerals Nutrients	Taste	Possible Side Effects
Mustard Greens	A cruciferous vegetable, mustard greens are cholesterol lowering, also full of a chemical compound called gluco-sinolate, which can help, cure certain types of cancer. Mustard Greens are also anti-inflammatory.	Full of vitamins K, A, E, B1, B2, B3 B6, C, E, fiber, copper, magnesium, tryp-tophan, potassium, folate, phospho-rous, and calcium	Slightly bitter	No known adverse effects
Parsley	Parsley is often thought of as a garnish but it is a great green juicing additive. It contains two types of volatile oil compo-nents—including *myristicin*, *limonene*, *eugenol*, and *alpha-thujene*. The second type is flavonoids—including *apiin*, *api-genin*, *crisoeriol*, and *luteolin*. Parsley is chemo protective and can prevent tu-mors. It also contains luteolin, a flavonoid that helps to clean the blood.	Folic acid, Vitamins B, C	Earthy, mild taste, can be slightly peppery	No known adverse effects
Purslane	Purslane is native to India and has been spread throughout the world from its original cultivation there. It is considered a wild weed but is very nutritious. It grows prevalently since it requires less water and soil nutrients than many other plants. It is low in calories but high in many important vitamins, trace minerals and essential nutrients. Its high antioxi-dant levels (especially melatonin) help to prevent certain types of cancer, and promote heart health.	High in vitamin A, Omega 3s, C, B-complex vitamins, and two alkaloids, (betalain) Also full of trace minerals like calcium, cop-per, iron, magne-sium, manganese, phosphorous, zinc, selenium, as well as folates	Mild, slightly sweet taste	No known adverse effects
Raspberry Leaf Greens	Raspberry leaf greens have been used for centuries to make medicinal teas. The leaves contain a natural astringent that help to cleanse the body. Raspberry leaves are also known to improve fertility in women. They can also help to regulate hormonal changes that accompany menstruation. The leaves can also help to promote stronger reproductive organs and muscles. This plant also helps with constipation, poor blood circulation, in-flammation, diarrhea, irritated skin, gum diseases, oral cavities, the cold and flu, respiratory infections, and other digestive issues.	Full of C, E, A, and B complex, minerals such as calcium, phosphorus, potassium, mag-nesium, iron and antioxidants.	Tender, sweet and tart	No known adverse effects

Name of Green	Health Benefits	Vitamins Minerals Nutrients	Taste	Possible Side Effects
Radish Leaves	Radish leaves are full of more antioxidants and important nutrients than the radishes themselves. Radish leaves have been used to treat kidney and skin disease as well as cure certain types of cancer due to a high levels of a chemical compound called anthocyanins. The leaves can even be turned into a poultice to help with insect bites.	Iron, calcium, B-complex vitamins, vitamin C, protein, and zinc	Mild to extreme peppery flavor	No known adverse effects
Spinach Leaves	Spinach is a great green juice additive. It has anti-cancer qualities (especially with prostate cancer) and is full of a special plant nutrient called glycoglycerolipids, which are what help the plant in its process of photosynthesis but also supports the cells of humans.	High levels of phytonutrients such as carotenoids (beta-carotene, lutein, and zeaxanthin) and flavonoids, Vitamins K, A, C, E, B1, B2, B3, B6, manganese, iron, selenium, choline, copper, zinc, potassium, manganese, tryptofan, and folate	Mild taste	No known adverse effects
Sunflower Sprouts	Sunflower sprouts have high concentrations of the mineral, zinc, which has been shown to improve sperm count in men. They also help support pregnant women due to high folate levels. Sunflower sprouts are a good source of plant-based protein, and are in fact considered to be one of the most complete sources since they contain all the essential amino acids. Sunflower sprouts boost the immune system and build the skeletal, muscular, and	High in folate, vitamins C, E, B, essential amino acids,	Mild taste	No known adverse effects

Get Your Free Bonus Below!

To get instant access to your free email course *"10 Days To Everlasting Health"* either click the link below if you are reading the digital version:

http://greensmoothies.me/freecourse

Once you sign up, you'll receive a daily lesson to your email, enjoy!

One Last Thing…
A Special Request
From Elizabeth

Thank you so much for reading my book. I hope you really liked it! As you probably know, many people read through the different reviews on Amazon before they decide to purchase a book.

If you enjoyed reading my book and feel like you've got some great tips and information about smoothies, could you please take a minute to leave a review with your feedback?

60 seconds of your time is all I'm asking for, and it would mean the world to me!

Thanks For Your Help!

Elizabeth Swann

Elizabeth Swann (Miller) has over 10 years of experience as a practicing Naturopath (ND) specializing in healing through nutrition. She has degrees both in Psychology and Naturopathy.

As a person struggling with overweight throughout her childhood, teens and early 20's, Elizabeth decided to take charge, take stock and start making changes in her life for the better. Her experiences with thousands of clients and her own personal experiences have led her to become an author. Her goal is to educate as many people as possible about the healing powers of food and how to easily incorporate these changes into daily life.

Elizabeth is happily married, has two beautiful daughters and currently lives and practices in Mount Carmel in sunny Israel.

Want to talk with Elizabeth? Email her at: Elizabethswannbooks@gmail.com
Visit her website at: http://www.greensmoothies.me
Discover more books by Liz by visiting: http://www.amazon.com/Liz-Swann-Miller/e/B009TPU68I/

Made in the USA
San Bernardino, CA
14 January 2014